Ever since I read *Stumbling toward Wholeness* by Andrew Bauman, I want to give a copy to everyone. Whether you are stumbling or marching, heading in many directions at once or confidently toward one, or looking for wholeness or who knows what—this book is for you. As you read it, you will realize you both stumble and march, you know what you long for, and you live with an inexplicable ache; and somehow, somewhere along this path, faith finds you. Do you have the audacity to consider the possibility of wholeness in this fractured world? Answer yes. Pick up this book. You are on the path to a radically new way of life.

SHARON A. HERSH, MA, LPC, bestselling author of *The Last Addiction: Why Self Help Is Not Enough*

What a bold, brave, and thoughtful reflection on the prodigal-son story. Andrew Bauman invites us into the drama and equips us to identify the feelings of shame, betrayal, contempt, and grief that we all wrestle with as we stumble toward wholeness. I came away encouraged by the boundless love of the Father for us all.

CRAIG DETWEILER, president of The Seattle School of Theology & Psychology

A few years ago, a friend of mine said, "We are at a time in the life of the church where stories of failure are much more important than stories of success." I couldn't agree more. And while that may sound counterintuitive, it shouldn't surprise us. In fact, what should surprise us is that our fascination with success stories has gained so much ground inside the church. After all, the Bible makes it clear that it is in our weakness that we discover God's strength; it is in our guilt that we discover God's grace; it is in our shame that we discover God's salvation; it is in our rebellion that we discover God's rescue; it is in our slavery that we discover God's freedom; it is in our failure that we discover God's faithfulness. This is one of the many reasons I deeply appreciate Andrew Bauman's book: It's real and it's raw. It's uncomfortably honest and therefore unfathomably hopeful. We need more books like this—books that acknowledge brokenness and need—for it is only then that we will see and appreciate the one-way love of God that comes our way minus our merit. Thank you, Andrew, for reminding me that "it is finished." I keep forgetting.

TULLIAN TCHIVIDJIAN, author of *One Way Love: Inexhaustible Grace for an Exhausted World*

This book takes a brave look at the story of the prodigal son and invites the reader to find true freedom in the loving arms of the Father. It calls us to embrace the resurrection that is found on the other side of repentance.

BRAD COOPER, pastor of direction and culture, NewSpring Church

Stumbling toward Wholeness is exactly what the title implies: It's Andrew Bauman's life, in process, shared beautifully and vulnerably with us as a gift. Yet, like any good story, it tells a larger story, imagined through the ancient biblical tale of a father and his two sons. It's his story and their story, but somehow it's also our story. And this is the beauty of Andrew's work. You'll be invited into the tears and laughter of a prodigious Lover who sees you, pursues you, and embraces you.

CHUCK DeGROAT, professor of pastoral care and counseling, Western Theological Seminary

Today I add Andrew Bauman's name to Luke, Nouwen, and Rembrandt as my beloved guides through the magical prodigal story from Jesus. Illumination is an ancient sacred practice. *Stumbling toward Wholeness* helped me anew to carry my grief, my shame, my confession, and my mourning, nudging me with its honesty and wisdom toward healing, joy, and hope.

TONY KRIZ, author of *Aloof: Figuring Out Life with a God Who Hides*

STUMBLING TOWARD WHOLENESS

How the Love of God Changes Us

ANDREW J. BAUMAN

A NavPress resource published in alliance
with Tyndale House Publishers, Inc.

NavPress is the publishing ministry of The Navigators, an international Christian organization and leader in personal spiritual development. NavPress is committed to helping people grow spiritually and enjoy lives of meaning and hope through personal and group resources that are biblically rooted, culturally relevant, and highly practical.

For more information, visit www.NavPress.com.

Stumbling toward Wholeness: How the Love of God Changes Us

Copyright © 2018 by Andrew J. Bauman. All rights reserved.

A NavPress resource published in alliance with Tyndale House Publishers, Inc.

The Team:
Don Pape, Publisher
David Zimmerman, Acquisitions Editor
Cara Iverson, Copy Editor
Libby Dykstra, Designer

Cover drawn by Libby Dykstra. Copyright © Tyndale House Publishers, Inc. All rights reserved.

Author photograph by Eratosthenes Fackenthall, copyright © 2017. All rights reserved.

For information about special discounts for bulk purchases, please contact Tyndale House Publishers at csresponse@tyndale.com, or call 1-800-323-9400.

Cataloging-in-Publication Data is available.

ISBN 978-1-63146-777-6

Printed in the United States of America

24 23 22 21 20 19 18
7   6   5   4   3   2   1

In dedication to my son, Jackson Brave Bauman,
and my sister, Julie McGill Bauman.
May these words honor my love and your legacy.

CONTENTS

FOREWORD

SINCE I WAS TWENTY-TWO, I have been exploring the question, *How do we become whole?* There is a theoretical impulse behind the quest, but what drives the search is the fact that I know that who I am is not who I am meant to be. I knew that before I knew the gospel, but in the early years, I shrugged off the inner war with diversions and addictions. I came to know the gospel, and one of the early stories that I surrendered to was the story of the prodigal son.

There was much about the Bible and Jesus that was foreign and unlikable to me. I may have become a Christian, but early on I wasn't that fond of my new faith or many of those who unquestioningly followed Jesus. Yet I was smitten by the story of the prodigal. I knew him intimately. The older brother was a fool, and I had known many like him. It took years for me to understand that the prodigal was a secondary character in the story and that the older brother and I were far, far more alike than initially seemed possible.

The character who allured me and terrified me was the father. I knew instinctively the story was fiction: There was no father like this in the ancient Near East or in the Midwest, where I grew up. But what if it was true? What if there really was a father like this character? Can a single story redeem one's hope in goodness? Certainly, one story can break one's heart. I began a relentless pursuit to explore the possibility that one story, three characters, and an improbable, compelling, disturbing plot—really a parable—can change the human heart.

Andrew Bauman has dared to take one of the core stories of the New Testament and set out on an epic journey to address the question, *Can the human heart really change?* His courage and wisdom is immense, and what he offers is life changing. One would think that after more than two thousand years of reflection on the gospel, we would have it down. We don't. In the same way, we have been attempting to answer the question, *How do we change?* And all answers are heuristic and incomplete. That is not a critique of this book or all efforts to engage the question. It is, in fact, a profound commendation of this book and Andrew's courage to explore a mystery that will always elude us even as it drives us forward.

Andrew has drawn from countless sources and imbibed the wisdom of those who preceded him. He has translated those stumbling forays into a new tongue and story, and it lights up the sky. Most of us know how to find the North Star. We know how to find the Big Dipper. And when I gaze up into the night sky and marvel at the stars, sometimes I am stunned by the splendor that surrounds me. This wise book will do the same for you.

Stumbling toward Wholeness will take you forward into your war of prodigal addiction and self-righteous envy. It will far-more expose your deepest desire to offer yourself and others the open-armed, lavish delight of the Father. His delight is our destiny—our greatest fear and our fondest hope. These three characters in the hands of a masterful storyteller such as Andrew can change your heart.

I have seen the waywardness of Andrew. I have seen the proud self-absorption of Andrew. And I have felt and received from him tears of delight and a welcoming embrace when I have failed him. What he writes arises out of his own search and the integrity to name what is true about his brokenness and the glory of his beauty. He understands all too well that it is only the true prodigality of the Father, Son, and Holy Spirit that gives us covering for our shame and restoration of our beauty. You will find this quest a life-changing encounter with the companions of this story. You will find Andrew to be a broken and beautiful guide for reading the night sky and finding the one North Star that will lead you home.

Dan B. Allender

ACKNOWLEDGMENTS

THIS BOOK COULD NOT HAVE BEEN DONE without the help of many. First, my wife, Christy, is a big fan of mine. Her support and belief carried me. Christy, I love you and I thank you for your sacrifice so this dream of mine could become a reality. Truly you are such a gift, and I am so blessed to have you as my partner.

Second, I stand on the shoulders of Dr. James Coffield and Dr. Dan Allender. Dr. Coffield, you have fathered me into the man I am today. Thank you for your help with this project and teaching me over the past fifteen years most of the contents within this book. You have saved my life, and I am proud to call you my friend. Dr. Allender, your guidance and teaching over the past ten years have been seeds planted deep within my soil. I am raising and cultivating all that you have given. Thank you—your impact on my family will be felt for generations.

Thank you, Traci Mullins, my behind-the-scenes literary

hero. I don't know how I would have done this without your guidance, wisdom, and support. I am honored that you are in my corner.

To the many friends, family, and colleagues who reviewed this manuscript about ten thousand times: Lisa Fann, Mike Anthony, Charlie Howell, Sharon Hersh, Mona Coffield, Rose Jackson, Wynn Archibald—I thank you all.

And finally, to NavPress. Thank you, David Zimmerman, for your editing genius. This book would not be nearly as good without your mad skills. Thank you also, Don Pape, for believing in this idea and giving a new author a chance.

I am honored and humbled.

May our good God be glorified in the pages ahead.

May God bless us with discomfort
At easy answers, half truths, and superficial relationships
So that we may live from deep within our hearts.
May God bless us with anger
At injustice, oppression, and exploitation of God's creations
So that we may work for justice, freedom, and peace.
May God bless us with tears
To shed for those who suffer pain, rejection, hunger, and war
So that we may reach out our hands to comfort them and
To turn their pain into joy.
And may God bless us with just enough foolishness
To believe that we can make a difference in the world
So that we can do what others claim cannot be done:
To bring justice and kindness to all our children
and all our neighbors who are poor.

— A FRANCISCAN BENEDICTION

SYNOPSIS OF LUKE 15:11-32

A Story of a Loving Father and His Wayward Sons

(a.k.a. The Parable of the Prodigal Son)

THE YOUNGER SON WAS READY—all set to make a life on his own (with his father's money, of course). He was breaking free from the doldrums of his youth and heading out to blaze his trail.

The father gave in, knowing that love works only by holding loosely. I wonder what the youngest son was feeling as he packed his belongings. Exhilaration? Terror? Hope? Was he seeking some deeper calling or fulfillment? A break to make a name for himself away from his father? Would this be his chance to finally begin the life he had always dreamed of?

He soon realized he had made a huge mistake. His new buddies stuck around only when he was financing their festivities. His empty wallet was his first indication that he was in trouble, and when things couldn't get any worse, they got much worse. A famine came over the land, turning the young son's dream into a nightmare. He was forced to turn his attention from matters of pleasure to matters of survival, becoming so desperate that he was envious of the pig's slop.

Suffering brought him back to his wits. It's one of those life lessons that we hate to learn and learn to hate. Heading back home a failure, having reached the point of near death, he was ready to give up. He began to practice a monologue of self-contempt, devising a plan to earn back the love he had frivolously squandered.

I wonder if the father watched for him every day. I imagine the father looking over the hill out the front window for any figure shaped like a man. How patiently he must have waited, filled with longing for his boy's return.

Then one day it happened. Somewhat like a UFO or unicorn sighting, the unconceivable became true. The father saw a staggering shadow in the distance. He ran with a wild, immodest abandon to his son. He held and kissed him, not wanting another moment to pass without the depth of his love being felt.

The son, perhaps becoming uncomfortable and knowing he was undeserving of such wholehearted love, delivered his speech: "Father, I screwed up. Let me work to replace what I took from you."

The father was too busy delighting in his son's rebirth to pay attention to the penance. He joyfully called to his workers to bring all the best goods—the fancy clothes, the leather sandals, the family signet ring, and the fattest cow they could find—enough to feed the entire village. He proclaimed that everyone must come celebrate the miracle of resurrection that had taken place.

Meanwhile, there was yet another son, his shirt still stained with sweat from his labors as he trudged toward the house from the fields. He had been managing the entire household all day and was anticipating a much-needed respite. As he got closer, he heard the ruckus coming from the house and asked a servant, "What is going on?"

"Your brother has come home!" came the reply. "It's time to eat!"

The elder brother's thoughts raced with accusation against his younger brother: *How dare he come home! How dare he eat the food that I labored over! How dare my father celebrate his rebellious child!* The elder brother seethed with anger and turned away, not wanting anything to do with this type of manipulation and deceit.

As the father partied, he wanted to share his joy with his entire family. Knowing that his older son was missing, the father went to the backyard and found his oldest son filled with bitterness. "I have worked so hard for you and never complained or asked for anything, and you have never given me squat. Now this traitor son of yours has wasted our wealth, and you respond by throwing him this colossal celebration?"

The father responded lovingly, "How could I not? When I thought he was dead, part of me died with him. But he is alive, and I feel alive again. I love him, and I love you." Because the father had known deep heartache, he possessed the capacity to experience boundless joy and invite others into what it means to be fully human.

INTRODUCTION

Stumbling toward Wholeness

MY FAMILY PUT THE "MENTAL" in fundamentalism. We weren't (and currently aren't) crazy; we were just broken. (Aren't we all?) My father was a lawyer and an insecure preacher, and my mother a pastor's shy daughter and an obedient woman who just wanted to have a biblical marriage and strong family. We acted as if we were the model Christian family, but beneath the surface, we were all dying inside. We had become buried underneath a growing pile of lie upon lie—the result of my father's addictions. We were focused on the family, the illusionary family, attempting to present perfection to the outside world, yet living shrouded in secrets. Truth was too difficult to confront, so we hid.

I was only eight years old when my parents split. I remember the white '86 Toyota minivan with brown racing stripes in which my mother carried my sixteen-year-old brother, my twelve-year-old sister, and my eight-year-old self from our home in Clearwater, Florida, to a "vacation" in the mountains of western North Carolina. I remember my father standing in the driveway weeping as I looked out the back window. My confusion as thick as my sense of loss, I asked myself, *Why is my dad not coming on vacation with us? He always drives the van on long road trips!* I was desperately trying to make sense of a world turned upside down.

After an eleven-hour drive, we arrived at our tiny blue rental house situated on several acres of farmland. It was nice and it was isolated. I remember walking by myself down the dirt road, in a daze, looking for friends—looking for myself—bored and forlorn. My older siblings didn't want to play, so I wandered, alone, feeling the burden of depression that was far too weighty for a little boy to bear. I was living inside a drama that was not my own, but I would bear the consequences. These consequences down the road would include my own sexual addiction and my wrestling with depression, anxiety, intense loneliness, and obsessive-compulsive disorder. Unaddressed woundedness always catches up to us no matter how fast and far we run.

All of us have "backstories" that have made us who we are. Whether our stories are joyful or tragic, ordinarily straightforward or hopelessly convoluted, we don't write our narratives when we are young; we live into what we are given. We are carried along, first one way, then another, until we arrive at the thresholds of the rest of our journeys. At times we choose courses of destruction, other times paths toward transformation. Either way, I believe we are stumbling toward God in an attempt to make sense of our wildly holy stories.

I didn't always have this view. The sermons of my child-hood focused almost exclusively on the sinfulness of people and neglected the mysteries of what grace and redemption actually mean. The main thing I took away was that I was a sinner. That made it easy to believe my own critical internal voices—or at least other people's voices of condemnation that I had picked up along the way and made my own—for example, my fourth-grade soccer coach, who called me "a lazy piece of crap"; or my eighth-grade science teacher, who insisted that I was "a slither-ing slug who leaves his grimy trail wherever he goes."

I was a lonely kid who was rarely pursued or engaged on an emotional level by any adult man. I was looking everywhere in my life to be fathered. I was never taught how to be a moti-vated, hardworking student, and I needed a thoughtful guide. I'm sure my teachers believed their criticism would propel me toward constructive action, but it only sent me deeper into shame and depression.

I'm sure you have voices of your own—curses that stay with you and go on to inform your inner world for the next thirty-plus years. These curses become our internal voices of self-contempt. There is a kingdom of darkness that uses those curses to mock and remind us that we are of little conse-quence at best or irredeemable at worst. I know that voice of darkness well. And I once heard it shouting from one of the most familiar and beloved stories in the Gospels: the story of the prodigal son.

I remember hearing my share of sermons about the prodigal son. Because of my self-contempt, I distorted this life-giving, love-affirming parable in Luke's Gospel into a message of condemnation. I focused on the rebellion of the wayward son and took it to mean that one's failures, mistakes, and problems are the defining aspects of one's soul. I thought of myself as the runaway son, unable to imagine my redemption. After all, I had been involved in so much sin already. This character fit perfectly with my view of myself. I knew I was bad, and my shame told me I did not deserve to return to my Father's house. I knew I had better accept Jesus into my heart or I would burn in hell forever. So I "got saved" seven times, just to make sure. But no matter how many times I was "washed in the blood," I still felt dirty. No matter how hard I tried, I could not be good enough, and feeling loved by my heavenly Father eluded me.

In the religious culture I grew up in, John 3:30—"He must become greater; I must become less" (NIV)—was used as gasoline to fuel my shame. Self-contempt was blessed as humility, and any love of self was labeled as haughty and self-centered.

What I know now, two decades later, is that the greatness of God is most fully realized and appreciated when we say yes to ourselves, when we consider our wholeness part of our sanctification. Although we cannot ignore the reality and seriousness of our sin, there is an inherent goodness to us that we must realize in order to become fully ourselves and completely reconciled to God. That's not to say that we aren't sinners; it's just acknowledging that we can't become "less" until we've become "whole."

German Catholic theologian Johannes Baptist Metz states, "Understood correctly, our love for ourselves, our 'yes' to our self, may be regarded as the 'categorical imperative' of the Christian faith: You shall lovingly accept the humanity entrusted to you! You shall be obedient to your destiny! You shall not continually try to escape it! You shall be true to yourself! You shall embrace yourself! Our self-acceptance is the basis of the Christian creed. Assent to God starts in our sincere assent to ourselves, just as sinful flight from God starts in our flight from ourselves."[1]

Assent to ourselves is not some humanistic, narcissistic plea to make God in our own image. Quite the contrary. This affirmation of the goodness of self simply takes seriously the fact that God has created us in his likeness. To live into who we are meant to be in God's family, we must wholeheartedly embrace the radical truth that we are image bearers of the divine, beloved by the God who created us.

When we recall that we are created in the divine image and that God looked on us and called us very good, we begin to realize the self-contempt that so often gets sanctified in our faith communities is actually a prideful stance: We unconsciously think that our self-hatred can cleanse us, that we can sit in God's place and forgive our own sin. We become consumed with self by unconsciously cutting ourselves down, sabotaging our own success, and isolating ourselves from life-giving relationships.

At other times, we have a puffed-up view of ourselves as "better than" because we try so hard to be righteous. We become indignant, self-pitying, and resentful when we don't get what we think is our due for good behavior. But secretly we fear being seen as undeserving. This is simply another distortion of the image of God in us.

I've come to understand that Scripture in general—and the parable of the prodigal in particular—informs us that all redemptive change begins when we see ourselves accurately, through God's eyes. When we deeply accept our Father's embrace, we will be neither self-rejecting nor prideful; rather, we will become humble and grateful. We will no longer be in bondage to self, justified in being self-indulgent, self-annihilating, self-loathing, self-righteous, or self-aggrandizing. Instead, we will see ourselves as God sees us and move into true freedom—to change, to serve, to love.

A JOURNEY TOWARD TRANSFORMATION

There may be an exact original audience and a specific original intent of the great story in Luke 15. There are great theologians who believe there is only one point and one way to interpret it. Those theologians may be right. This cherished parable has been studied by people far more knowledgeable than me. However, one of the beauties of teaching in story (parable) is that each culture, each generation, will inevitably find fresh nuances and additional meanings hidden within the Master Teacher's story. A good story does more than just tell the facts; it is evocative and reveals truth.

I am not the first to come to the conclusion that the

characters in Luke's narrative are present and inter-
acting within each of us. Henri Nouwen's *The Return of
the Prodigal Son* is based on his observation of Rembrandt's
famous painting depicting the father, son, and brother in
this story. Rembrandt captures with precision the younger
son's exhaustion, the elder brother's disparaging gaze, and
the father's wholehearted embrace.

Nouwen's reflections on the painting take him on a journey: At times he identified with the younger son—"feeling
quite lost . . . homeless and very tired." At other times he
could relate best to the older brother: "For my entire life I
had been quite responsible, traditional, and homebound.
. . . I saw how much of a complainer I was and how much
of my thinking and feeling was ridden with resentment."[2]
Nouwen ultimately embraces the idea that he is to be like
the father: "For a long time the father remained 'the other,'
the one who would receive me, forgive me, offer me a home,
and give me peace and joy. The father was the place to return
to, the goal of my journey, the final resting place. It was only
gradually and often quite painfully that I came to realize that
my spiritual journey would never be complete as long as the
father remained an outsider."[3]

I had never seen the story through this lens. I was stunned
to realize that the runaway son, the judging elder son, and
the gracious father all have warred within my bones. The
rebellion of the son, the judgment of the brother, and the
love of the father battle for supremacy inside me. Obviously,
my own story and understanding of transformation influence

my interpretation of the parable, but I don't think I stray from the truth when I say that the story of the prodigal son, elder brother, and father is the story of us all. Indeed, each of us possesses these three personas, and we have to somehow reconcile them to one another.

As a result of reading Jesus' parable of the prodigal with this approach, my work as a psychotherapist, my spiritual practices, and my journey toward seeing myself the way God does have changed dramatically. This journey has required courage and a willingness to look deep within to address the obstacles to living in the Father's embrace. I write with a conviction that self-reflection and devotion to God not only can coexist but also can flourish together.

Some Christians have come to believe that turning inward for healing is a self-serving, godless endeavor. Yet I have found on my own healing path that by bringing a posture of prayerful contemplation to the process of self-examination, I come to know God much more fully and intimately. God is *in* us: "Do you not recognize this about yourselves, that Jesus Christ is *in* you?" (2 Corinthians 13:5, emphasis added). "God . . . was pleased to reveal His Son *in* me" (Galatians 1:15-16, emphasis added). And we are meant to experience this peculiar grace that creates space for God to make his home in us. This integration of God within is what is meant by assent to self. And this is good news for those of us trying to make sense of our lives, attempting to become healthier individuals and lean more fully into the mystery of who God is in ways that truly change us.

A ROAD MAP FOR THE JOURNEY

The problem with writing a book based on the parable of the prodigal son is that many of us grew up hearing this story again and again, which is another way to say that we have never heard it at all. The familiarity of the parable can actually block us from living its deep truths fully, or even for the first time. However, if we return to Jesus' story with a soft heart and an open mind, inviting the Holy Spirit to accompany us, we will see that each of the characters in the parable is alive and constantly at work inside us, moving us toward transformation.

I have found it helpful to imagine that each character in the parable represents a realm of our being. We are designed by God to dwell in the realm of the father, where love and mercy abide, but most often we lose our way as we traverse the shame-strewn realm of the son and the contempt-strewn realm of the elder brother.

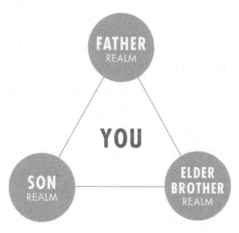

The Son Realm

When we live in the Son Realm, our ultimate goal is relief from our pain. We are driven by avoidance of heartache, pursuit of relief, and escape into pleasure. The prodigal son left the relationship with his father to pursue counterfeit forms of comfort and pleasure. He ended up in a place of shame, addiction, and isolation. Like the son, we all struggle with shame and self-contempt as ways to help manage the pain of our pasts or our current unpleasant realities. We fear our own hunger, our ravenous need for love and intimacy, yet we continue to choose the safety of separation.

In this realm the pull is to act like a victim and remain powerless to change. In the process of transformation, moving beyond the Son Realm requires that we explore our unhealthy attachments and addictions and make peace with our shame. We must embrace our inherent God-given dignity as image bearers and beloved children of God and turn ourselves toward home.

- **GOAL:** Relief

- **FELT STRUGGLE:** Shame/Self-Contempt

- **PULL:** Victim

- **CORE FEAR:** Hunger for Love

- **RESULT:** Isolation

- **WHAT DRIVES US:** Avoidance of Pain/Pursuit of Pleasure

- **WHAT WE MUST ADDRESS:** Self-Rejection and Core Dignity

We are all runaway sons and daughters, caught in cycles of self-destruction, either blatant or subtle. We struggle with allowing ourselves to be unconditionally loved by others and by our gracious Father, who welcomes us home. We must confront our shame narratives because they push us further away from God's plan for our healing.

The Elder Brother Realm

All of us are not only the son but also the elder brother. The runaway's brother stayed at home and worked his father's land, but he was motivated by duty rather than love. It is easy to hijack the true gospel with performance-based righteousness. This posture makes us feel "holier than thou" and gives us the illusion of control. But similar to the prodigal, it is a search for pleasure, relief, and survival—just attempted differently.

In the Elder Brother Realm, we must face our sense of entitlement: the belief that we deserve God's blessings because of our good behavior. We must wage war against the harsh judgment and contempt we are inclined to feel toward others. We all carry a harsh judge inside ourselves. This judge is insecure, yet self-aggrandizing; entitled, yet so full of self-loathing that he condemns in others what he cannot bear within himself. Beneath this rage is a deep well of sadness and a sense of loss and betrayal. The elder brother is just as lost as his younger sibling. He feels that his hard work, dutiful spirit, and good behavior should be his ticket to the party, but they are the very things that block him from the inclusion he was meant for.

Whether male or female, each of us is the elder brother at times. Our goal when we find ourselves in this realm is our version of justice. We want what is "right," too often at the cost of mercy and grace. This fierce sense of self-righteousness makes us feel powerful. However, when we are in this realm, we also feel vulnerable, and our core fear is being exposed as "not good enough after all." We become prideful in order to cover up our fear of being wrong or "less than." When faced with betrayal and deep pain, it is much easier to rage than to enter into grief. It is all too easy to lash out at others to escape the war within.

- **GOAL:** Justice

- **FELT STRUGGLE:** Entitlement

- **PULL:** Power and Righteousness

- **CORE FEAR:** Exposure

- **RESULT:** Others-Centered Contempt and Judgment

- **WHAT DRIVES US:** Comfort

- **WHAT WE MUST ADDRESS:** Pride and Insecurity

The Father Realm

It is easy to stagnate in the realms of the son and the elder brother, yet deep inside the heart of an image bearer of God is the hope that this is not where the story ends. This hope moves us slowly toward the third realm, where we can begin to experience God's unfathomable love and delight.

In stark contrast to the realms of the son and elder brother, the goal in the Father Realm is full restoration and healing. The father demonstrates many of the traits we are called to integrate within ourselves.

When we enter the Father Realm, our tasks are to befriend grief, extend kindness toward ourselves and others, and surrender control. The pull is for us to be like God in our kindness, but we must address our core fear of potential rejection. In the parable, the father has already been left and rejected by his youngest son in favor of the son's need to explore. And though he hopes his son will return, he will never know if his son is returning for money and provision or because of a genuine desire to reunite with him and his family. The cost of living in the Father Realm will be vulnerability to increased pain but also capacity for deeper celebration. In the Father Realm, there is always great risk in great love. As the parable displays, the father is at risk of his son's continued withholding of love. In order to open his heart and extend unconditional love in the face of past and potential relational pain, the father must give up control and make himself vulnerable.

However, the Father Realm is where God's face is clearest. The father boldly grieves his younger son's apparent death and his older son's blindness to steadfast love. This posture of courage is one we are all called to imitate, because the deeper we allow ourselves to risk pain in relationships, the more capacity we have to experience joy. The father's gracious love toward both sons shows us there is space to offer unconditional love to our own shame, contempt, entitlement, and judgment and to extend this grace to others. If we can join the father in this radical kindness toward our own and others' sins and failures, no longer judging but allowing God's kindness to guide us, then we, too, can experience restoration and celebration.

- **GOAL:** Restoration and Healing
- **FELT STRUGGLE:** Embracing Grief/Kindness to Self and Others/Surrendering Control
- **PULL:** Kindness
- **CORE FEAR:** Rejection
- **RESULT:** Celebration and Resurrection
- **WHAT DRIVES US:** Willingness to Risk
- **WHAT WE MUST ADDRESS:** Issues of Control

RETURNING HOME

The story of the prodigal son and his family depicts wildly good news: No matter where we find ourselves on our journeys, God (the father in the story) loves us as we are and longs for connection with us. This is true whether we are the self-centered, self-despising prodigal or his self-righteous, demanding brother. Unconditional love is actually what it says it is: without condition. God delights in us, period.

The righteousness granted by the Father through the work of Christ is greater than any past, present, or future failure and shame.

Learning to recognize the realms in which we are inclined to dwell can deeply influence our journeys of inner healing, strengthen our relationships with others, and deepen our bonds with the Great Healer. Sometimes we will find ourselves or those we are walking alongside in more than one realm at a time. The process of healing is not a straight line and is never completely finished. Change takes time, and we have to develop kindness and patience as we wait for the stubborn part of ourselves to catch up with what our minds know is good. Whether we relate more to the wayward prodigal or to his hard-hearted brother, readjusting our view of ourselves as the father's beloved "sons" and reclaiming our language toward accurate self-understanding is the birthplace of meaningful change. Joining the Father in how he views us launches us on a journey toward transformation, dismantling self-contempt, shame, and entitlement and affirming God's extravagant delight in us, his cherished creations.

In my own quest to make sense of my story, my understanding of God has become clearer and kinder, and so have I. My family has courageously undergone much transformation as well. And though it takes crucifixion to get to resurrection, we have learned that the more we live in truth, the more we experience God. Looking back at myself as a little boy and looking at my life now, I realize that I was and currently am on a quest to return home. I am seeking rest and refuge—a safe place in a world that often feels confusing and unkind.

My prayer as we explore and rediscover the classic parable of the prodigal son is that you, too, will return home in the most profound way. When we know both our greatest depravities and our highest glories, we can celebrate the goodness and wholeness of redemption—not because we have escaped suffering, but because we have lived to tell our stories of shame, betrayal, and reunion. I hope you will allow the pursuing, suffering, sacrificing love of God to entice you to move beyond shame, contempt, and entitlement and on to grief, kindness, and transformation. If you are feeling stagnant, may you be disrupted. If you are in need of comfort, may you find peace. If you feel exhausted, may you sense the breath of God at your back as you take in the words of Jesus. May you experience God's grace that breaks the curse of condemnation and know the love and delight of the Father who lives within you.

Whether you are at the beginning of your healing journey or years down the road, my hope is that this book can be a gracious and supportive companion on your treacherously splendid pilgrimage back home.

PART ONE

TRAVELING TO THE FAR COUNTRY:
THE RUNAWAY SON

- **GOAL:** Relief
- **FELT STRUGGLE:** Shame/Self-Contempt
- **PULL:** Victim
- **CORE FEAR:** Hunger for Love
- **RESULT:** Isolation
- **WHAT DRIVES US:** Avoidance of Pain/Pursuit of Pleasure
- **WHAT WE MUST ADDRESS:** Self-Rejection and Core Dignity

CHAPTER ONE

BATTLING AFFECTIONS GONE MAD

*Addiction is not the problem. Addiction is
the attempt to solve a problem.*

GABOR MATÉ

*Even though you get the monkey off your back,
the circus never really leaves town.*

ANNE LAMOTT

*[Jesus] said, "A man had two sons. The younger of them said to his
father, 'Father, give me the share of the estate that falls to me.' So
he divided his wealth between them. And not many days later, the
younger son gathered everything together and went on a journey
into a distant country, and there he squandered his estate with loose
living. Now when he had spent everything, a severe famine occurred
in that country, and he began to be impoverished. So he went
and hired himself out to one of the citizens of that country, and he
sent him into his fields to feed swine. And he would have
gladly filled his stomach with the pods that the swine were
eating, and no one was giving anything to him."*

LUKE 15:11-16

DURING MY SOPHOMORE YEAR OF COLLEGE, I was flunking out
of school. Drugs, alcohol, and sex kept me numb enough
to survive, but I knew I needed a change of environment to
remain alive. I packed all my belongings in the back of my
'89 Isuzu Trooper and moved from my apartment on campus

to live in a small tent about seven miles from the school in what was known as "pocket wilderness" in the East Tennessee Mountains. The woods felt safer than the hyperconservative college I attended. The woods didn't judge me for my tattoo, earrings, and untamed appearance. It held my tears and doubt with kindness. I remember long days sitting by the river, skipping class and soul writing, praying to something or someone for help, craving a new life and yet not knowing how to get one.

Even in the darkest of days, I heard whispers of God in those woods. He continued to woo me to the life I was seeking, but my loneliness was by far the loudest voice I heard in this season of running away.

One afternoon I decided to return to campus to check my mail. I met eyes with a resident director about thirty feet ahead of me. I smiled and nodded; he did the same. I was happy someone of influence saw me and acknowledged my presence and was pleasant. He walked toward me as I gathered my mail. He was actually going to talk to me; I was so lonely, so hungry for connection, that my heart leaped.

His first words were "I'm going to have to give you a demerit for wearing shorts in this building." I had forgotten that I had shorts on instead of the required long pants (it was eighty degrees outside). My smile quickly changed to shock. He had no way of knowing that just the other day I had held a gun in my hand, imagining how the bullet would pass through my brain. This is exactly why I had run to the woods for safety. His one sentence killed something in my heart: He was more concerned with my behavior and following the rules than about my very life.

Why was I breaking the rules? Why was I acting out? We often hope that our internal struggles will be evident to others. I was lost and needed Christ's people to locate me, to see my face and kindly name what they saw. I wanted him to say, "I haven't seen you in a while—I have missed you" or "How are you really doing? You look sad." I longed for his eyes to be soft and his heart open to listening to my untold stories, to truly love me instead of judging and dismissing me. I know he thought he was just doing his job, yet he missed a divine opportunity to love me at a desperate time in my life. His lack of acknowledgment and kindness seared my heart. I was breaking the rules and acting out because I wanted to literally get "caught"—to be held and known by someone larger than myself.

We often miss the desperate pleas of others. In an attempt to do what is "right," we miss the heart of Christ's command to "love one another" (John 13:34). That was my last semester at this particular institution, and though I continued to struggle with my identity and place in God's story, I was thankful to get out of that season of desperation alive. I continued to stumble forward, seeking folks who would be able to enter my pain with wisdom and care.

I (and all of us) bear a trajectory similar to that of the son in our parable. A litany of addictions, deep-seated shame, extravagant living, wasteful spending, and sexual promiscuity—these and other forms of sabotage in our lives represent a rebellion from what is good, a sprint away from love, a fear of hope, an exodus from the glory available to us.

GETTING BENEATH THE SURFACE

There's a popular saying: "We should focus on the sin beneath the sin."[1] The behavioral sin on the surface is often a symptom rather than the core problem. In the church, more damage has been done by deep relational sin than by surface behavioral sin.

Relational sin is simply a refusal to love; it's the choice (at times unconscious) to use, betray, or commodify an image bearer of God. Jesus seems to suggest as much in the Sermon on the Mount. He seems to say that behavioral sin is not of primary importance; more important in the Kingdom perspective is the relational sin beneath the behavior. When we treat a person poorly, the core sin is not the bad behavior per se, but the disregard of the person's dignity as an image bearer of God.

Most of us have little problem admitting our sinfulness. Our failures can be easily recognized. Many times, though, we focus on the *what* of sin instead of looking more deeply into the *why*. Sinful behavior can be an easy target that allows us to ignore a condition of the heart that needs tending. Because we feel unworthy of love, we move away from healing and consequently are more likely to harm others. Sinful behavior, then, can be both symptom and side effect of brokenness.

I don't know what started the movement of the prodigal son away from his home, but I know that his travels to the far country started with a decision to push away relationship and love and journey toward comfort and false intimacy. He operated under the illusion that he could do life by himself, on his own terms. The truth was that he had the means to travel and party only because his father liquidated his assets.

The hearers of Jesus that day would have been astounded by this story. No one would ever treat his or her father that way. For the prodigal to ask for his inheritance early (before his father's death) was equivalent to "wishing his father *dead*."[2] So this is our first glimpse of the father: a demonstration of sacrificial love. When his son makes his outlandish request, the father honors it at great cost to himself, both in terms of finances and in terms of his reputation. But the son wasn't thinking about sacrificial love; he was seeking a comfortable life, running from responsibility and relationship.

We run from all sorts of things. When my parents were in the beginning of the end of their marriage, I decided to run away. I don't know whether I was reacting to the tension in our home, overhearing arguments, or just feeling an overwhelming fear that my entire world was no longer safe. I loaded my small backpack with vital provisions of graham crackers and juice boxes, went out on the back porch, and turned left to find a small break in the fence that I was able to crawl under. As I hid in the nearby woods, it was weirdly comforting to hear my parents frantically searching for me, though I had been gone for only a couple of hours. It was as if I needed to know that I mattered, that they would try to find me. As the sun began to set, I returned home to the tearstained face of my father. I remember my surprise when I saw my absence had affected him.

We rarely grow out of the temptation to escape to places of comfort and release. Many times children are more authentic in acknowledging their pain, and we as adults must learn to listen and see. Our adult forms of running away can look quite different from those of childhood, but they are actually not that different at all. As a child, I just packed my bag and walked out of my family chaos, while as an adult, I stayed quiet and escaped through addiction.

ADDICTION

The energy behind running away is a commitment to relief and a refusal to sorrow and struggle. Addiction is one of the most common manifestations of escape from self. We see this in the prodigal-son story as he depletes his resources and a famine overtakes the land. With his resources gone, he finds himself lost and desperate, looking for something to connect with and belong to. He attaches to the countrymen who give him a job, but the job is unsatisfactory (our wrong attachments will never give us enough of what we want). We then find him hoping to eat the pods he is feeding the pigs. The hearers of this story would have known of this food, thought to be carob pods that are sweet but not satisfying, and incapable of sustaining human life. The picture of the young, lost orphan longing to eat what would not satisfy him is a vivid picture of addiction.

Henri Nouwen wrote, "I am the prodigal son every time I search for unconditional love where it cannot be found."[3] One of the most significant ways I embodied the runaway son was my search for love in my thirteen-year addiction to pornography. I come from the first generation where anyone old enough to click a button could access pornography.

I was twelve when my family first got dial-up internet in my home. My friend Steven was an excellent teacher; he showed me how to search for naked women and erase the history so our parents wouldn't find out. We knew how to use the computer better than our parents, and this new uncharted nude world at our fingertips was always accessible and incredibly exhilarating. We were not afraid of getting caught, as we had become masters of deception and had internalized our shame. Within a few days of finding my new hobby, I had seen more naked women than my grandfather had in his entire life. I felt alive.

We will always be drawn to life, whether that is genuine life offered by God or its counterfeit. During the years I was addicted to porn, I had long seasons of sobriety at times. I had accountability partners and belonged to men's groups. I prayed ten thousand times for God to remove temptation— for him to forgive me, or at least show me mercy and make me a eunuch. But I was still addicted, and it was a horrible struggle. Nothing worked. God remained silent, and I could never bring myself to the knife.

My use of porn began as an innocent curiosity. Since there was so much silence in our home concerning sexuality, I needed to find answers, and Steven had them. Sadly, those "answers" slowly began to grip my life with a steady clinch, and my curiosity turned habitual. I would make sure my mom and siblings were gone and go into the sanctuary of the computer room to soothe. My computer screen remained lit, I still liked naked women, and shame bound me more and more.

All affections in the far country work this way. It's not hard to imagine that the prodigal in Jesus' story tried to find satisfaction in money, shallow friends, popularity, and sexual promiscuity. When life becomes all about self and when the energy of life is about relief from our self-imposed hunger for true connection, then love becomes manipulation, strength becomes cowardice, and dignity becomes arrogance. Pornography addiction is a perfect example of this. I stopped seeking intimacy with a real-life partner who could have the power to hurt me. While using pornography, I didn't have to consider the needs of a partner, as it was a completely selfish act, whereas genuine love is about giving and receiving pleasure, a shared human experience of goodness.

Evil is that thing that is set against God and, because we are created in God's image, is set against us. Evil is self-propagating, emulating God's creative work in its own destructive effort, committed to steering us away from love and toward lesser things. Whenever we find ourselves ensnared in addiction, we can, if we are careful and diligent, discover in it a godly desire turned upside down. So driving each of our affections gone mad is a God-instilled longing for beauty, strength, hope, relationship, and delight. In other words, there is a deeper desire driving our addiction. What we need and want, what we are made for ultimately, is relationship.

In Jesus' telling of the prodigal parable, we are not privy to what the son was after, specifically. Was he searching for fulfillment of longings he could not satisfy at his father's table? What was keeping him from connecting with his father's love? Jesus doesn't tell us, but because his parables are intended to cause us to reflect on our own journeys, we might surmise that the prodigal both craved and feared intimacy, as we do. The young son struck out on his own to find life apart from owning his deep longing for connection and relationship with his father.

This was true in my prodigal journey. Running toward pornography addiction was actually the closest thing to heavenly connection that I could access at the time. My family had been devastated by my father's infidelity, which led to a formal severing when my parents split. My pornography use started after my parents' separation, as I longed for some form of relief and beauty in the desolation of my life. I ached to be touched, to be held, to feel pleasure, and to numb my pain. Pornography met those needs, as any addiction does for a time, but it never answered the deepest questions of my heart. Behind the thin veneer of each of our stories is a common thread of hoping for genuine connection and sabotaging any chance of it. In fact, says therapist and author Dan Allender, "Every addiction is an attempt to slay hope."[4]

This is not just the banter of a therapist trying to justify his own poor choices. In the late 1970s, Bruce K. Alexander, a psychologist, noticed this curious connection between addiction and relationships. He saw that rats kept isolated in cages would inevitably become addicted to the numbing chemical offered them, choosing water laced with morphine over tap water. However, when put in a "rat park" full of other rats (relationships), toys, and activities (healthy pleasure and playful delight), a significantly lower number of rats would choose the numbing substance and become addicted.[5] In humans, this connection was noticed with Vietnam veterans. Many would take heroin in Vietnam to self-soothe and escape from the horrors of war in a faraway land; however, most would discontinue heroin use as they reentered their normal world full of relationships and families.[6]

It seems that the story of the prodigal son is teaching us what science is just now coming to understand: It is relationship that drives us, damages us, and heals us. Until we discover how we have moved away from relationship and toward false connections and name what we truly crave (authentic intimacy), we will be stuck, much like the prodigal lost in the pigpen.

MOVING TOWARD REDEMPTION

The prodigal will never leave the pigpen by focusing on only the sadness of his desire for the "pods," like leftovers instead of a meal. If he focuses on only his disgraceful position, he will never risk the shift for something better. The prodigal rejects relationships and community and commits himself to selfish living. He wastes his money and it runs out. Any friends in his new community do not seem to stick with him after his money is gone. There is a famine in the land, leading to further trouble and despair. One of the signs of addiction is to continue one's behavior despite the consequences, and his change in fortune did not change the prodigal.

There is a great ironic twist of shame in the story. Pork is a forbidden food for Jesus' audience, yet here is the Jewish boy feeding pigs. The young man has gone from being full of confidence and having money in his pocket to being lonely and defeated, feeding the livestock and desperately needing reprieve. The same pigs that were restricted from his diet became his companions, and he envied the food they ate. Hearers of this parable knew it to be a tragic tale, but Jesus knew that addiction and shame were not the end of the prodigal's story. In the eyes of the storyteller, this was the beginning of redemption.

Addiction and shame are not how our stories have to end either. But to move toward hope, we must face our false dependencies, not just keep telling ourselves lies such as "Just one more time" or "It's not that bad" or "No one is getting hurt." When caught in addiction, we lose sight of the great and noble purposes for which we were created. The evil one hates any design that enables us to reflect the glory of God. In fact, John tells us that the evil one came to "steal and kill and destroy" (John 10:10). We creatively collaborate with the evil one's schemes to destroy us in various ways. Addiction can blind us. We may not notice that we need more and more of something to get the desired relief. When our false source of relief is not available, we become desperate or experience withdrawal; in other words, if we stop our addiction, we pay a price. The reward system in the brain is rewired as we crave more and become satisfied with less. But remember that under each of these desires gone mad is a godly longing that must be owned. That godly longing is the goodness and restoration God has in store for us.

Addiction is only one manifestation of running away and escaping our desires. We may not have the classic "loud" addictions of substance abuse or sex, but few of us avoid the much more dangerously subtle ones. Our relationships with food, work, or achievement, for example, can serve the same purpose as heroin for a drug addict. In either case, the drive is for escape from our own terrifyingly holy desire for authentic connection. We fear this much more than we'd like to admit.

Pornography had me in its grip because it offered a relatively risk-free mirage of intimacy without the relational risk of rejection. My true desire for authentic love seemed too daunting, and I settled for the cheap imitation rather than having the courage to suffer for the return home I was made for. Fortunately for me and for you, our stories don't have to end in the pigpen. But to move toward hope, we must face not only our addictions but also the inevitable shame that accompanies them.

DISCUSSION QUESTIONS

How have you interpreted the parable of the prodigal son in your own life?

In what ways has your journey been similar to the prodigal's, if only in subtle ways? How have you moved away from relationship and toward false connections?

What consequences can you identify from your attempts to satisfy your soul with something other than relationship with the Father (for example, addiction, shame, self-contempt, isolation)?

What purpose has been served by your own pursuit of pleasure or avoidance of pain? Can you identify the deeper longings that might lie beneath "running away"? Name some of the fears that have driven you to run from authentic connection. What is one example of how this is playing out in your life today?

CHAPTER TWO

EXPOSING OUR SHAME

Shame is a hemorrhage of the soul.

ATTRIBUTED TO JEAN-PAUL SARTRE

Every saint has a past, and every sinner has a future.

ATTRIBUTED TO OSCAR WILDE

I will arise and go to my father, and I will say to him, "Father, I have sinned against heaven and before you. I am no longer worthy to be called your son. Treat me as one of your hired servants."

LUKE 15:18-19, ESV

AFTER RUNNING AWAY FROM HOME, and after our subsequent battles with addiction, we enter the shame that follows. Shame keeps us bound to our addiction, separating us from our true homes and lasting change. This shame whispers lies that we are dirty, unlovable, incapable of dignity, and undeserving of mercy. These messages confirm why we got addicted in the first place, and they keep us in our distant countries, far from home.

In Luke 15:19, the humiliated son stutters to his father, "I am no longer worthy to be called your son. Treat me as one of your hired servants" (ESV). The son has come to believe that his sin and shame are his truest identity. He now trusts that he deserves the company of swine or, at best, the lowly status of a servant rather than his father's acceptance and love.

Despite its dire consequences, shame can be a comfortable place for us to reside. Shame contributes to not only addiction but also a multitude of other mental health concerns, such as post-traumatic stress, depression, suicidal tendencies, anxiety, eating disorders, violence, and oppression.[1] When we live in the shame of the Son Realm, we are unable to envision the father's welcoming love. We are "bad" and we know it, so we subsequently live out what we believe to be most true about ourselves. This foundational lie must be addressed if we are ever going to taste the fullness that God intended for us to experience.

One of the greatest deceptions we have come to believe is that we *should* feel shame for what we have done. But Scripture teaches that shame was ultimately taken away through Jesus' sacrifice on the cross (see 2 Corinthians 5:21; Colossians 2:13-15; Hebrews 10:12-14). Although guilt feels entirely appropriate when we have a foolish lapse in integrity, shame should no longer rule our lives. We must untangle these two feelings to get clearer views of ourselves and our Savior.

Researcher Brené Brown defines shame as "the fear that something we've done or failed to do . . . makes us unworthy of connection. . . . *Shame is the intensely painful feeling or experience of believing that we are flawed and therefore unworthy of love and belonging.*"[2] She goes on to state, "I don't believe shame is helpful or productive. In fact, I think shame is much more likely to be the source of destructive and hurtful behavior."[3]

I have found this to be true in my own therapeutic practice. Shame is both devastating and complex, and it hijacks the transformation process. If a client is experiencing a high level of shame, my ability to get close is inhibited. My questions and pursuit of his true heart are blocked because shame tells him to hide at all cost, not allowing his true self to be seen or known. In her 2012 TED Talk on shame, Brown says,

Shame drives two big tapes—"Never good enough"— and if you can talk it out of that one, "Who do you think you are?" The thing to understand about shame is, it's not guilt. Shame is a focus on self; guilt is a focus on behavior. Shame is "I am bad." Guilt is "I did something bad." . . . Guilt: "I'm sorry. I made a mistake." Shame: "I'm sorry. I am a mistake." There is a huge difference between shame and guilt, and here's what you need to know: Shame is highly, highly correlated with addiction, depression, violence, aggression, bullying, suicide, eating disorders.[4]

Research connects shame with feelings of unworthiness, subservience, and powerlessness. While guilt offers an opportunity to change one's actions, shame is an attack on one's core selfhood.[5] The prodigal son did not understand this reality, and it is where the church today often continues to fail. We have believed the lie that feeling ashamed can help redeem us. In reality, it pushes us further from the transformation that we seek.

In the early stages of writing this book, as I asked colleagues, friends, and friends of friends to review it, I remember one of them defending the concept of shame: "You will want to be careful not to completely dismiss shame as wrongheaded. There is a place for shame that drives us to the cross. Sorrow for our sin is an important part of repentance." This particular editor was extremely helpful in some ways, yet I knew from this statement that she could not distinguish guilt from shame.

Guilt (and its cousin embarrassment) are *adaptive emotions*. Though these emotions are common, they normally do not interfere with everyday activities. (I am aware that many times people are considered immobilized by guilt and are called guilt ridden; I would argue that these folks are actually shame ridden.) Shame is *maladaptive*, meaning that our typical responses while entangled in shame are flight, fight, or freeze.[6] When we deal with shame in unhealthy ways—denying it rather than acknowledging it—psychological development is inhibited, and shame materializes in destructive behaviors such as addiction and self-contempt. Shame not only keeps us from returning home but also hinders our ability to realize healing change. Guilt can legitimately convict us of sin, but shame cuts straight to the core of our self-worth and leads only to increased hiding, addiction, silence, and self-loathing.

Once we have unbound shame from guilt, we can trace our shame stories and begin restorative journeys. We can recognize our shame by first identifying what we are most silent about. What stories do you choose not to tell? Where do you hide your face? Where does your voice change when you speak? Do you disassociate or check out when you hear a certain type of story? When do tears come? All these questions provide data to help you uncover where your shame might be located.

I remember watching the movie *Finding Nemo* with some friends when it first came out. Halfway through the film, I was struck by the amount of tears I was trying to wipe off my face. I was embarrassed at first and attempted (unsuccessfully) to resist my body's need to get something out. This film stayed with me (the grief and desire are still palpable even as I write this), and it took me years to realize why that movie pierced my essence so profoundly. *Finding Nemo* might as well have been called *Finding Andrew*. I was a young man who so desperately yearned for his father to pursue him. The mere sight of watching a father (yes, even a cartoon-fish father) so passionately pursue his boy was part of my most intimate holy and good longing. I was watching my desire portrayed on the screen, and the most honorable response was for me to obey my body and weep.

We must continue to be aware of what moves us. Any shame, heartache, or desire brought to the surface must be tended to with kindness and care. And as God would have it, this path to healing is intended to be taken in the context of community.

SHARING OUR SHAME

Identifying our shame is the first step toward reconciling with it. The next step in healing our shame is to share these stories that so slyly bind us.

I facilitated a workshop on addiction a few years ago, and as it was nearing a close, I fielded questions from the audience. Someone asked a question along the lines of "Have you as a professional ever struggled with your own addictions?" Maybe it was less direct than that, but I was presented with an opportunity to break my silence, to step out of hiding for the first time with people I sensed would embrace me in the midst of my shame. From my experience with clients who had honored me by sharing their shame stories, I knew that inviting a safe person into the places where self-condemnation prevailed would be liberating and healing. With trepidation but hope, I admitted to a roomful of strangers that I had been addicted to internet pornography. I had never confessed my addiction out loud, except within the confines of therapy.

When the words left my lips, I nearly lifted my hands in an attempt to grab them and wrangle them back into my mouth. In a panic, I said to myself, *What have I done?* But then I began to feel something wash over me: a divine and holy kindness, like baptismal waters washing away my shame. Maybe that is what the Holy Spirit feels like. In a place where I had always held self-contempt, kindness snuck in without my permission. The shame lifted and I was able to own my story publicly for the first time.

As I scanned the room, looking for expressions of judgment and disgust, I found none. What I did find were soft eyes full of tears and kindness locked onto mine. Their faces were gentle, their bodies leaning in toward mine as

I continued to share a condensed version of my addiction journey. Even though I had spent years in therapy engaging my shame and experiencing a modicum of healing, this terrifyingly sacred experience of self-disclosure turned out to be the most liberating of all, not only for me but perhaps also for my listeners. Spiritual teacher Marianne Williamson wrote, "As we're liberated from our own fear, our presence automatically liberates others."[7] I had been released from my fear, from my shame and self-hatred, and because of that freedom, others began to feel the same release. Many folks came up to me after the workshop and thanked me for my courage.

To make sense of the healing that took place when I told my shame narrative, I turned to theologian Frederick Buechner's memoir *Telling Secrets*. Buechner writes,

> The God of biblical faith is the God who meets us at those moments in which for better or worse we are being most human, most ourselves, and if we lose touch with those moments, if we don't stop from time to time to notice what is happening to us and around us and inside us, we run the tragic risk of losing touch with God too.[8]

I truly think that in that moment I was able to honor and engage my shame with courage and kindness because all of us in that room were able to experience a small piece of God. When we break the silence of our shame, it loses its power to define us. God is truth, and when we live in truth, we experience God.

Author and anthropologist Zora Neale Hurston once said, "There is no agony like bearing an untold story inside you."[9] I can picture the prodigal son as a grown man, possibly with children of his own. I can imagine him sharing his story as a gift to those around him: entering his shame narrative of squander, telling of his addictions while he was away from home, and describing his glorious return to his gracious loving father. I envision him naming his failures, his strengths, and his decision to receive the goodness of his father's love. When we do this type of redemptive story-telling, we reclaim good from evil, exchange shame for glory, and bring light to previously dark places of our souls.

Sadly, finding a safe, caring community that is rooted in vulnerability can be a difficult task. Many times I have felt safer in a twelve-step group than in the sanctuary of a church. Bringing forth stories of shame and guilt has long been welcomed in twelve-step groups, while churches have often been uncomfortable with these concepts.

My own church did not seek to help me understand my father's addictions or my own. I began regularly attending Al-Anon meetings across town when I was a youth pastor. Al-Anon is a safe and caring place for people to process problems that come with having addiction in one's family. I remember feeling the desperate need to attend the meetings and a heavy weight being lifted off my chest after each one. Al-Anon was life giving in a way that my church family did not know how to be at that time. In Al-Anon I felt far less alone in processing the chaos of my father's addictions.

Where do you find authentic places of engagement and comfort for your shame? The church I currently attend does a good job of holding my doubt, my pain, and even my desire not to be there at times. How does your church community hold you when you are not well? Do you feel you have to be something you're not? Do you feel you have to put on a mask so you will be accepted? If that is the case, you are probably not in a safe, caring community; you are in a comfortable social club that massages your propensity to hide from your authentic self.

The beauty of a twelve-step program is that oftentimes the people in meetings are desperate and have given up pretense and are too tired to fake it anymore. Frederick Buechner writes about the beauty of Alcoholics Anonymous:

> No matter what far place alcoholics end up in, either in this country or virtually anywhere else, they know that there will be an A.A. meeting nearby to go to and that at that meeting they will find strangers who are not strangers to help and to heal, to listen to the truth and to tell it. That is what the Body of Christ is all about.[10]

Alcoholics Anonymous is not the only place for authentic community, but it is a group that helps communally facilitate the healing journey. It is a beautiful model of how we should position ourselves when we come through our church doors.

What would it mean to start offering authenticity among those in your community? Would you consider inviting a few close friends to start your own caring group? When you share your own desire for authentic connection, others can admit they long for it too. Step into your fear and pursue that desire. The sharing of your narrative has abundant power to transform the heart of both the teller and the hearer.

That said, there are people who may not be ready to receive or hold the beauty of your heartache well. Your story of shame is a gift—a sacred pearl. Jesus says, "Do not throw your pearls before swine" (Matthew 7:6). Be careful about choosing whom to share your story with, as there is great potential for unintentional harm.

I remember my client Tammy telling me about sharing her sexual-abuse story for the first time with her mother. Brilliantly and courageously, she described her sexual trauma, caused by the neighbor boy, that had haunted her for years. Her mother's first response was, "I thought something weird was going on with that boy, but your dad and I just kept praying for you!"

I almost fell out of the chair when Tammy shared her mother's response, but she didn't think twice about it because this was the type of careless engagement she had experienced her entire life. I asked her to read what my face was telling her. She said, "Well, you seem both surprised and disturbed." I applauded her for reading my face well and asked if she would explore why I felt this way about her mother's response.

Over the next forty-five minutes, we untangled the bonds of shame around her orphaned heart and unpacked how she had wished her mother could grieve alongside her. Despite her parents having the best intentions of prayer, there were no conversations in their household concerning her sexuality, no discussions about her growing body or changing hormones. Even though they had suspected "something weird" was going on at the neighbor's house, they had never engaged in dialogue about that weirdness. Tammy was unintentionally set up by her parents and then left to deal with her sexual abuse on her own.

Tammy's grace toward her mother was greater than mine. We discussed the courageous story that she brought to her mother, the failure of her mother to respond appropriately, and her mother's inability to own her own guilt for failing to protect her daughter's precious body. Yet Tammy was patient and wise and knew the core goodness of her mother. She exhibited a resilience in her vulnerability that was beautiful to witness.

A few weeks later Tammy approached her mother again, this time telling of her disappointment that her vulnerable story was not held well. Tammy had to address her anger at not feeling protected by her parents. This time her mother was able to hear her, grieve with her, and be with her in the disappointment in a nondefensive and profoundly loving way. Tammy felt heard, loved, and held, and part of her heart was healed in the moment of shared grief.

I know that this type of nondefensive response is rare and sadly not the norm when it comes to confronting those who have harmed us or not held our stories tenderly. I want to make clear that our healing is not contingent on the person we are telling hearing us and holding our shame story well. That is codependence and emotional enmeshment, not healing change. Our healing is contingent on our courage to engage our own stories, even if someone else's cowardice prevents him or her from entering the stories with us.

We must have wisdom in regard to whom we choose to confide our stories. We must guard our vulnerable hearts at times despite how strong our desire is for reconciliation and love. People must earn the honor of hearing our stories and be able to hold them with soft hands and full hearts.

In the parable, we see the son suffer without anyone to hold his story well once the money ran out. "No one gave him anything," we read in Luke 15:16 (NLT). Clearly, their motives were not to love and be in relationship with the son but to use him for their own gain until he was no longer of use to them. Later in the parable, we see the picture of redemptive story sharing in the way the father held his son's broken story well, by seeing and holding out hope for the resurrection in it.

Who do you journey through life with? How do you know who is safe to share your stories of shame with? Who knows the most glorious and darkest places of your soul? Who are the kind and strong characters of your stories? I was able to share my story of pornography addiction because after years of therapy and internal work, I was in a place of strength where I was no longer controlled by my shame or defined by my sin. Yet it took another couple of years before I was able to share that same story with my own mother. It was much easier for me to tell it to strangers than to the mother I had longed to engage me during that dark season.

The reason we are timid about sharing with those closest to us is that there are real consequences if the interaction does not go well. I was thankful that ultimately my mother was able to hold my story of sexual brokenness well. I felt heard and loved.

Psychotherapist and relationship expert Dr. Robert Masters offers a helpful caution: "Shame left unattended, shame left in the shadows, is shame that will run us from behind the scenes, disempowering us and determining far more of our behavior than we might imagine."[11] One of the chief benefits of pushing into our vulnerability and learning to share our stories of shame is that when our stories are shared, we can release the control we have unconsciously allowed shame to have over us. Another benefit of sharing our shame narratives is finally allowing our bodies a chance to release all they have been holding. Shame and the body are deeply connected.

RELEASING SHAME FROM OUR BODIES

"Crawl inside this body—find me where I am most ruined, love me *there*," writes poet Rune Lazuli.[12] Scripture tells us that our bodies are good and precious to God—so good that he chooses to rest, reside, and play within us. The apostle Paul writes, "Do you not know that your bodies are temples of the Holy Spirit, who is in you, whom you have received from God? You are not your own; you were bought at a price. Therefore honor God with your bodies" (1 Corinthians 6:19-20, NIV). Fat or thin, sweaty or clean, broken or whole, God accepts us. Whether we have a history of sexual abuse or not, God delights in us.

But because our bodies house the spirit of our Creator, evil craves to annihilate our bodies, either through the abuse perpetrated by others or our own cruelty against ourselves. Our bodies are the vessels that contain our stories, so in order to release our shame narratives, we must learn to listen closely and compassionately to our bodies. Often our shame narratives are held in specific parts of our bodies. To locate embodied shame, we must kindly take inventory of where the stories are lodged. What is the story of your nose? Your penis or your vagina? What about your breasts? Your stomach? Your thighs? Your ears? Where does your body bear shame?

When I was in tenth grade, in the locker room after gym class, I had on only my shoes and boxers and thought it would be funny to run around dancing in my underwear and being silly. My buddies laughed, and we were having a good time acting foolish until my penis fell out of the hole in the front of my boxers. My friend Shawn saw my penis and started laughing, mocking its size. He started telling all the other guys in the locker room about it, and my unabashed joy turned into searing humiliation. I remember turning back toward my locker and getting my clothes on as fast as I could. I defended myself and fought back my shame, but for the rest of that day, I felt red faced and vigilant. How much had the gossip already spread to the two thousand other students in the school? Did the people talking around me know? What did they think of me? Did they laugh as well? I remember two girls approaching me in the hallway after fifth period, asking if I was "small down there." High school can be a brutal place.

This story still affects me. When I go to the gym and change in the locker room, I notice how I turn my body away from everyone's view and get dressed as quickly as possible. Even thinking about exposing my body in a locker room causes my heart to race. I need to practice kindness and soothe my anxious heart whenever I reexperience my adolescent shame. Even after a decade of entering my field of work, I still find unexplored places and resurfaced memories that require my attention and care.

My friend Heather's story of shame revolves around her pinky. Yes, her pinky. Even our tiniest parts can hold shame and must be addressed. I asked Heather to share a bit of her story:

> My left pinky is very crooked and has been since
> I've known it. I didn't think too much about it
> other than some occasional fascination until I
> reached junior high. There isn't a specific incident,

but even so, it became one of many body parts in
my pubescent inventory that was imperfect and
noticeable. I was a girl burgeoning into womanhood
amongst boys attempting manhood, and their focus
seemed to be solely on the body: how big the breasts,
how long the legs, how soft the skin, and, truly, how
appealing and normal the bone structure. I recall the
looks of disgust from some of the boys for anything
out of the ordinary. Consequently, my pinky grew
less fascinating to me and more embarrassing. I hid
it for fear of being teased or creating disgust.

Pubescence can be the cruelest of stages. Heather was not
only taking her own bodily inventory but also comparing
and contrasting her body with her peers, measuring what
normal is against what the social paradigm defined. The insecure "boys attempting manhood" became kings of scrutiniz-
ing anything out of the ordinary, and Heather was left to
internalize the messages that were being given. The shame
of her pinky was beginning to allow a larger, darker narrative
that she herself was unworthy. This is how shame works: It
slowly corrodes what is good into something disgusting.

Heather continues,

My crooked pinky was shameful, and when that
experience of shame situated itself in my heart,
I placed all kinds of proverbial alarms on this small,
delicate finger. If there was a potential sight of it, my

mind rang with sirens, and I would quickly disguise
it by putting it in my pocket or bending my fingers
toward my palm. This was happening even ten
years later when I landed at a charismatic church in
which they often lifted their hands during praise and
worship. I refused to lift my left hand up, and if I
did, I found a way to slide my pinky in front of my
ring finger, safe from the danger of ever being seen.

Heather is a beautifully wild woman. To hear her war
breaks my heart, yet I am struck that she had the integrity
to give her beautifully holy pinky the credit it deserves. Her
pinky has been holding the rivalry of good and evil.

Before you dismiss my claim as hyperbole, consider that
even in worship Heather attempted to hide her pinky finger's
inadequacies. Many times we neglect the shame our bodies
hold rather than letting them tell us what they need. Our
bodies tell the truth. As you listen to your body and realize it
does bear shame, what do you do? How do you reclaim your
good body from shame?

Psychiatrist and researcher Bessel van der Kolk, in his
book *The Body Keeps the Score*, says,

> Traumatized people chronically feel unsafe inside
> their bodies: The past is alive in the form of gnawing
> interior discomfort. Their bodies are constantly
> bombarded by visceral warning signs, and, in an
> attempt to control these processes, they often

become expert at ignoring their gut feelings and in
numbing awareness of what is played out inside.
They learn to hide from their selves.[13]

We must listen to the truth that our good bodies are softly
whispering. Listening is a way to redeem the trauma of searing shame our bodies have bravely endured. Heather's story
is a beautiful example of this.

In my counseling practice I help clients listen to their
bodies by leading them through a prayerful centering exercise
of embodiment. I first ask them to close their eyes, firmly
place their feet on the ground, and become aware of their
breath, breathing deeply and slowly in through their noses,
followed by an extended exhale through their mouths. Then
I ask them to describe what emotions they are feeling within
their bodies and where those emotions are being held. A common emotion is shame. After the shame is located, I ask my
clients to continue to take deep breaths while placing their
hands gently where their bodies are holding the shame. Then
we must get underneath the shame to see what drives it, so I
ask about what their bodies are saying in regard to the shame
they discovered. This is the point where the body must tell
its own story. Here we can start the process of making peace
with the shame that has historically ruled us.

One client working through this exercise located a sensation in her right ankle. I trusted that her body was guiding
us to something that needed to be told, and we continued to
explore what this sensation in her ankle was. She realized this

was the exact spot on her leg where her primary perpetrator had grabbed her right before he assaulted her. Her ankle continued to hold the trauma even after her mind had blocked it out for more than thirty years.

With centered silence and intentional care, we can begin to hear the cries of our bodies' stories and start to reclaim what evil has tried to steal from us. Even the smallest parts of our bodies that bear shame must be addressed so evil cannot develop strongholds within us.

A CASE STUDY ON EMBODIED SHAME

Sam woke up in a cold sweat, tired from the mental war he had just fought and terrified from the shame he had just come face to face with. The dream was so vivid: Katy was there with her husband, standing outside the auditorium of their old university, and Sam knew he needed to see her, talk to her, apologize to her for how he had harmed her so many years ago.

Thankfully, that morning Sam had his men's group. They routinely talked about their various addictions, stories of heartache, and haunting shame. He felt safe to share his dream and the story of shame behind it, but many men that morning were eager to catch the group up on how they had been doing, and some brought difficult stories to address. Sam just sat there, squirming with nearly an unbearable amount of shame. The more he sat and waited, the more his hands began to shake, his legs wobbled, and his breath both deepened and lessened simultaneously. His heartbeat quickened, and he placed his hand on his chest as an attempt to care for the shame that had been activated. He was pregnant with his shame: Labor pains were increasing, and his body was breaking open. Shame was pushing out of him whether he liked it or not.

If we are in tune with what our bodies need, they will always tell us the truth and lead us into what we need to confront within ourselves. God resides in the body; he speaks to us there. Sam allowed his body and dream to matter, and as he listened they were able to communicate what he knew he needed to address in his story.

When the leader of the group finally called on Sam for his routine check-in, he nearly erupted, telling the men of his shadowy dream. He spoke of his fear of facing and confronting the sin he had perpetrated on Katy in college. He told the group the story of when he continued to push Katy sexually further than she felt comfortable with and how he had eventually sexually abused her. He began to weep and confess what he felt was an unforgivable sin. He began to enter into the shame his body had been bearing for nearly twenty years.

What Sam did was incredibly immoral and sinful, yet by holding the shame in his body for decades instead of addressing his pain, the enemy got exactly what he wanted. The way evil twists sexual sin can debilitate both victim and abuser, and the way to undo that shame is through coming into deeper communion with our own bodies.

Sam sat in the center of the group, closed his eyes, and

imagined Katy sitting in front of him. Guided by his therapist, he spoke with her. He wept bitterly, never before allowing himself to face her, even in his imagination. Sam apologized for his selfish behavior that harmed her, said he was sorry for pressuring her beyond her boundaries. Then, with his therapist's instruction, he looked up, holding the gaze of the other men in the group. The men's eyes were soft and kind, not judgmental and condemning as he had expected. Sam's breathing regulated and his body began to relax into itself. The therapist then asked the other members in the group to reflect to Sam what they saw in him. "Courage," "integrity," "strength," "forgiveness"—the men spoke bold truth in ways Sam could begin to hear for himself because he respected them so much. Though this was only the beginning of Sam's healing journey of his sexual shame, the group members were correct that he showed immense courage, strength, and integrity in facing his sin and allowing the voice of God within his body to be his guide.

Our bodies are meant for God, not for shame; yet our bodies have carried shame for far too long. In order to pass through the Son Realm and into the Father Realm, our stories of shame must be thoroughly explored. This shame we have held within us has led to our silence, isolation, and addiction, and where that shame resides is where we need love, kindness, and redemption (the Father Realm) most of all. We must have the guts to tell our stories of shame to compassionate sojourners in a way that removes the power of evil and eradicates shame's ability to turn into self-contempt.

DISCUSSION QUESTIONS

What stories do you not tell? What stories are you silent about?

Where in your life have you confused shame with guilt?

Where have you tried to escape the shame in your own story?

Are there places within your body that hold your shame?

To whom can you give your stories of shame?

Do you have a community of story sharers? If not, how can you begin to develop a circle of trusting sojourners? If so, where do you all need to continue to push more deeply into your narratives of shame that hold you captive?

CHAPTER THREE

CONFRONTING OUR SELF-CONTEMPT

My enemy said to me, "Love Your Enemy."
And I obeyed him and loved myself.

KAHLIL GIBRAN

Treat me as one of your hired servants.

LUKE 15:19, ESV

Here they stand,
Lining both sides of the sidewalk as I stagger forward.
My thirty assailants' posture proud and unshakable,
    waiting for my arrival.
Their fists pound the air with anger over my head,
    their voices loaded guns pressed cold and firm against
    my brow. "You are stupid," "You will never make
    something of yourself," "You are fat," "You are clumsy,"
    "You are lazy."
They continue to shout. I pretend not to hear their
    lashings. I put my hands over my ears and look straight
    down, hoping my hands will speak kind words, that the
    concrete will offer me peace.
Yet I hear them still, now muffled only with more
    bass. Their voices shake my core.
"You are a bastard child," "You are just like your father,"
    "You are not ready to be a husband," "You will be an

absent father," "You are a coward." The voices of self-
contempt shake my core.
With each syllable riddling my chest like bullets, I am
bleeding from the inside out.
I am a dead man walking. Where can I find silence
between my ears?

I WROTE THIS POEM after years of battling with intense periods of self-contempt due to unresolved shame. The voices inside my head condemned my every move, picking apart each story of shame with accuracy and precision that cut deeply. Each accusation felt all too true. At times the voices crippled me with anxiety and self-doubt, making it difficult to even be alone with myself.

In the Son Realm, we must address our propensity toward self-contempt, the tendency we all have to make war against ourselves because our shame tells us we deserve condemnation. Many psychologists and sociologists define self-contempt as the "inner critic"—the judge inside ourselves that watches us through a lens of harsh self-judgment. It is important to note that self-contempt is not just low self-esteem; it is much darker than that. Therapist Andrew Ide defines self-contempt as "an active, degenerative, languaged presence within us that seeks to nullify goodness."[1] Therapist Chuck DeGroat describes the inner critic as "at worst . . . a 10 foot tall monster within, attacking us with accusations, and no doubt prompted by the Accuser himself."[2] The evil one hijacks our inner monologue and uses self-contempt as a way to "steal and kill and destroy" us (John 10:10).

As our unaddressed stories of shame lie dormant within us, self-contempt begins to metastasize, and our shame becomes even more multifaceted. The shame marinates, and it eventually "becomes internalized in the form of the inner critic."[3] In other words, if our unaddressed shame invites evil onto the porch of our lives, then self-contempt is the doorway that enables evil to take residence. The evil one ("the father of lies," John 8:44) commandeers our shame and begins to twist it into something much more covert and diabolical. Evil convinces us that our self-judgment is warranted. This voice of evil has an edge to it that is condescending, condemning, and disparaging but sprinkled with enough truth to bring immense confusion.

For the younger son, shame and self-contempt morph into an inner voice of condemnation when he comes to his senses in the pigpen and realizes how far from home he is. Reading the text at face value, it is clear that he wants to return but believes he is "no longer worthy" (Luke 15:19) to be called his father's son. He thinks he deserves the worst from his father, to be treated as nothing more than a servant in his own home. This critical voice causes him to lose vision of what it might be like to return to full communion with his father. "Make me small, Father," the prodigal requests, "because that is how I feel on the inside."

Like the young son, we project our self-contempt onto God and others: "I hate myself, so he/she/they must hate me too." As a result, self-contempt keeps us separated from relationship and inhibits deeper healing. The interplay of shame and self-contempt can be sneaky in another way as well. Andrew Ide further describes how self-contempt can "work" for us in the face of our shame:

> Contempt often serves to temporarily restore equilibrium. We may, somewhere within us, desire healing and justice for ourselves and others, but contempt is far more readily available. Fundamentally, contempt is an escape from feelings of guilt, shame, powerlessness and helplessness— to survive experiences that feel *God-less*.[4]

In other words, turning against ourselves can be easier than entering difficult emotions. Making villains of ourselves helps us escape the grief required to fully engage the healing process. All self-contempt creates barriers against the transformative power of love.

OVERCOMING CONTEMPT FOR OUR BODIES

Just as with shame, contempt for our bodies is a particularly dangerous battleground in our war with self-contempt. In my clients, I often see a deep contempt for the tender places within themselves, especially in the way they view their bodies. Those vulnerable places are most commonly associated with and blamed for their past traumas.

I remember working with a client regarding an intense scene of sexual abuse she suffered some thirty years earlier. Sarah began by telling me of a first date and the excitement of going out with a very attractive firefighter. She was only eighteen; he was twenty-two and had a nice truck. She described to me how delight turned to horror as she was date-raped by this man she was attracted to.

I sat with her in silence, my heart breaking at what she said. Then, after about ten seconds of silence, I saw her head slowly begin to shake from side to side as she said aloud, "Why did I wear that white dress? I should have known better not to have worn that dress."

I was shocked at her confession, yet not surprised. She had unconsciously blamed herself, as most victims of sexual abuse do, and still did, even after all these years.

I knew I had only a few seconds to react, to attempt to disarm the power of her self-contempt. I said, "You wore that white dress because you desired to look beautiful, and that man not only didn't honor your beauty, he tried to destroy it." She had turned against her very *desire* to be beautiful and made her desire itself evil. It was easier for her to blame herself and her desire for beauty than to hold the perpetrator responsible for the evil he committed against her.

With tear-filled eyes I continued to name this truth on her behalf. "Sadly, this scene has more to do with his perversion than your dress. He marked you, and this is a heartbreaking story." The truth was the opposite of what her self-contempt told her: Her desire to be beautiful was a glorious yearning, not something to be condemned. She couldn't hear me at that time, as she was not quite ready to let herself off the judgment seat. Yet this was the beginning of going to war with her self-contempt.

Sarah's story departs from the prodigal's, as Sarah had no culpability in the shaming event that fueled her self-contempt. Nevertheless, it is a good illustration of the power self-contempt has to block us from reconciliation—in Sarah's case, from a loving relationship with herself. It is no coincidence that most of our work for the next year was the healing of her self-hatred and the condemnation she had declared against her own body. She initially sought out counseling with me because she was struggling with depression and anxiety, along with difficulty maintaining intimate relationships. Yet those presenting issues were just masking the unaddressed wounds from her sexual abuse. The voice of evil twists the truth of our traumas to make even the most innocent feel at fault. Sarah had joined evil's attempt to destroy her and had made herself the villain of her story.

This is where we can differentiate between the heinous sin against Sarah by her abuser and the sin of self-contempt that Sarah continued to perpetuate on herself well after the abuse was over. Evil had twisted Sarah's abuse narrative so as to perpetuate the harm against her. Even though her abuser was long gone, she had internalized his violence and made it her own. Sarah is not and will never be responsible for the original violence against her, but she is complicit in the harm she continues to do to herself.

What does Sarah get out of blaming herself? She gets to escape (for a brief moment) from the heartache of her sexual abuse as well as her longing for beauty in relationship. Her self-contempt is an effective flight from the abuse, or at least an attempt to minimize its impact. Even though her life is in ruins because of continually running from and denying the result of the abuse, the fear of confronting it is too commanding. If she tells the truth of what happened, it will become more real, the visceral response will feel excruciating, and she'll experience the emotions of powerlessness and betrayal all over again. Yet that is exactly where she must go: toward the monster, toward what is most terrifying in her story.

The same was required of the prodigal. We don't know precisely what the younger son was feeling, but it is interesting that rather than weeping at the feet of his father (and the father then weeping along with him), the younger son says, "Make me your servant!"

Which might have been a safer posture for the son—repenting and allowing his heart to break in the presence of his father, or condemning himself in the presence of his father in an attempt to appear repentant? Which decision would have kept his heart from being broken open? Judging himself might have been far less painful, far less vulnerable than facing his longing for connection and reentering a loving relationship with his father.

The stories that bear the most fear and shame hold the most power and control over our lives. Until Sarah names the truth of what happened that day, until she declares herself the victim of a brutal crime and the man as the perpetrator, she will continue to be bound by her abuse, self-contempt, and loyalty to the voice of evil. When she comes to bless her beauty, honor her innate goodness, and stop cursing her good body, she will begin to experience the freedom of God's transformative work.

What about your own precious body? Will you delight in your body's goodness the way God does—the curvature of your nose, the magnitude of your ears, that acne that never seems to go away? God delights. Do you mock the size of your penis? The dimensions of your breasts? Those stretch marks? God relishes his masterful artwork. It seems quite bold to mock something God is so pleased in, to scoff at the fine art of the Master Creator. In order to honor our bodies and heal stories of shame, we must give the reality of spiritual warfare the credit it deserves. Our bodies are the front lines for good and evil, and we must first uncover how shame is lodged within our bodies so we can reclaim them from the evil one. What if spiritual warfare for you is standing in front of a mirror naked, apologizing to each body part that you have had contempt for? What if fighting evil means touching, blessing, and praying for each body part that holds shame, asking God to increase your loving-kindness toward that particular feature so you can dislodge the shame that resides there?

I remember a time when I cursed my own precious body. I was standing with my friend Ben at the park, watching our kids run wild at the playground. We were talking about getting our dad bods back in shape after a particularly cold and rainy winter in the Northwest. I remember making a comment about my butt getting fat, being able to make unique flapping sounds with my new love handles, and needing to get my six-pack back. That was it—just a quick jab at my waistline and booty to get a cheap laugh from a friend. What came next shocked me.

Immense guilt swept over me. I had mocked my body and knew I was wrong in doing so. I had made fun of myself in a demeaning way, and it felt as though I had entertained a dark spirit. I have made fun of myself a lot over the course of my life, but after years of therapeutic work concerning my self-contempt, I had made a commitment to honor my good body—the body that has worked so hard to heal from its own trauma. I had vowed to treat my body and soul with holy kindness.

My guilt riddled me. I repented. In a determined act of spiritual warfare, I said to myself, *I am sorry, body. You have served me well and done an excellent job. I should not have disrespected you in that way, and I am sorry. You are beautiful and deeply good.* And I said to God, "I am sorry for how I treated your beautiful creation. What you made in me is worthy, good, strong, and quite stunning. May I have the courage to join you in your delight of my body. Amen."

To journey toward change, we must first make a commitment to be on our own teams. The world is cruel enough without us. To become an advocate for oneself, to speak words of life to oneself, is to join God's delight and enter the Father Realm.

We tend to read the parable of the prodigal son as a story

of sin, repentance, and restoration. That is perhaps the primary meaning of the parable, and it has rewarded reflection over millennia. But what if there are journeys other than sin journeys that the parable exemplifies? What if reading the parable as a sin story doesn't go far enough? In what ways does the parable preach the gospel to our deep-seated shame over the wrongs we have done *and* the wrongs done to us, including the ones we do to ourselves? What if God doesn't want to just restore us from our sin but also deliver us from our shame?

It seems clear to me that the prodigal's father wanted nothing more than the restoration of his relationship with his son. Rather than shame him upon his return, he showered him with holy kindness. I believe we are called to do the same to our shame-bound souls.

THE POWER OF KINDNESS

Shame and self-contempt always stop growth and block healing, yet how often do we treat the tender places within ourselves with violence without thinking twice? We abuse ourselves, mock ourselves, and create a fear of our vulnerability.

But we *can* change those critical voices. Proverbs 18:21 tells us, "Death and life are in the power of the tongue." We have the opportunity to change the "death" meaning of our stories by the power of our tongues. To breathe "life" into those places of fear and shame, we must do so through kindness.

To treat our tender places inside with compassion may seem difficult at first. The messages that play in our minds are mostly the ones of past suffering and sin, which are always twisted, toxic, contemptuous messages that have led us to where we are currently: lost and confused and full of displaced rage. We have the power to create new messages and replace contempt with blessing, with the voice of God rather than that of evil guiding us.

For example, my four-year-old son is learning how to ride his bike. He started out on a balance bike and now is attempting a pedal bike; he's been struggling to get it down. As he begins riding shakily, he most likely will fall. Imagine he topples to the ground and begins to cry. I could engage him in a couple of different ways to attempt to teach him to ride:

1. I could use *contempt.*
2. I could use *kindness.*

Pay attention to what is happening in your body as you imagine my using contempt to motivate my son: "Son, what are you thinking? Can't you figure this out? Get up and stop crying, you little baby! Suck it up, be a man, and do it again!"

If that represents my son's experience of learning to ride a bike, how will he ride from then on? He will learn to ride, but most of all he will learn to be timid and terrified of my violence. He might never ride free again. He might never enjoy the liberation that riding a bicycle offers. My contempt might traumatize him and steal the essence of goodness that is riding a bike. As he grows up, he might develop his own inner critic (an echo of my voice in his own head), especially when learning new things. He may develop a perfectionism that guards him against the contempt of others and struggle to find his worth in performance-driven activities (an unconscious reenactment of trying to earn my love). This may sound extreme, but I have heard more stories like this than I care to remember.

Imagine that we all have a formative four-year-old inside us attempting to learn something new, watching us learn how to act and live. Most of us are asked to accomplish things as adults that we are expected to know, yet no one ever taught us. We do not know how to properly engage the timid four-year-old inside our own hearts.

How do you parent the child inside you? Do you engage the young, tender parts of yourself with kindness or contempt? With rage and demandingness, or with mercy and grace? Sadly, I too often find contempt more easily accessed than kindness, and with each verbal lash of the whip, I push my tender self further underground and away from the kind man I pretend I am.

What would it look like if I engaged my beautiful son with kindness as he learned to ride his bike? As he fell, I would come alongside him with my arms open to hold him. "Son, I am so sorry you fell. That looked like it really hurt. How about I stand next to you and hold the bike next time as you learn to pedal? Let's practice in the grass first so if you fall again it will be a much softer landing. I wonder what happened last time you fell that we can work on together." I can imagine the tears in his soft eyes slowly drying as he nervously walks back toward his bike, but only because he knows he doesn't have to face the daunting challenge alone. My kindness will now accompany him. If I engage my son with this compassion, he will learn not only how to ride but also to love it. He will be empowered and liberated to ride wildly, freely, and confidently.

How do you speak to yourself when you fall? Where is the kindness in your voice to the tender places within you? What if you parented the young or wounded parts of yourself with the same tenderness and kindness of a loving father or mother rather than with the contempt of your inner critic? How can you come alongside yourself as you grow into the man or woman of God you have so longed to be?

We don't know for sure whether the prodigal son ever became kind to himself and broke the cycle of his self-contempt, but he was able to reenter intimate relationship with his father, and self-contempt and authentic intimacy cannot coexist with ease. They are oil and water. Through the wild, persistent love of a father, all defenses eventually break down.

SELF-CONTEMPT'S IMPACT ON RELATIONSHIPS

Self-contempt not only violates ourselves and the image of God that we bear but also destroys the potential of an intimate relationship. First John 4:18 says, "There is no fear in love," but self-contempt is ultimately rooted in fear—fear of our insecurity being exposed or our being unchosen. Self-contempt isolates, leaving us alone and longing for something more. Even though on the surface it might look as though we were hurting only ourselves, self-contempt is a sin that affects all those who love us, because it shuts people out.

Let's say I sin against you. I have been gossiping about you to a mutual friend. The news gets back to you that I have been denigrating you and mocking you because of your impish disposition. You immediately come to me with your complaint and hurt feelings and confront my cowardice and betrayal. Let's say I apologize to you. For example's sake, I will apologize to you in two different ways. On my first attempt I will apologize with self-contempt present, and on the second I will apologize without self-contempt. (It may be helpful to imagine yourself actually receiving these apologies and noting what your body feels as you hear them.)

- **APOLOGY #1:** My friend, I am so sorry I said that about you. I am such a piece of junk. I was such an idiot to say that about you. I am sorry I was so stupid. I hope you can let it go and forgive me.

- **APOLOGY #2:** My friend, I am so sorry I said that about you. I have failed you. I should not have said that about you. I betrayed your trust as a friend and, worse, embarrassed you in front of another friend for my own selfish gain. My hope is that over time I can regain your trust and mend what I have broken.

CONFRONTING OUR SELF-CONTEMPT

As the offended party receiving the apology, what do you feel? In the first example, would you have wanted to move toward me? Would you have wanted to reconcile with someone so manipulative? Do you feel prone to care for me because of how I am beating myself up? The self-contempt in the first apology made the entire reconciliation process about me and how bad I was rather than about how I harmed you.

Self-contempt is fundamentally a form of covert narcissism. What I am actually telling you beneath my manipulative jabs at myself is that I am more ashamed that I got caught than sorry about how my words may have affected you. My first apology pushes you away from me and makes it difficult for us to repair the relationship. It also makes it much harder for you to properly forgive the sin I have committed because I am more contemptuous than contrite. A cheap forgiveness for the sake of superficial harmony is not the same as true restoration or reconciliation.

In contrast, the second apology pulls your heart toward mine. You actually want to forgive me because you know I am sincere. I did not turn on myself but felt and owned my sin against you. I made my second apology about my sin against you and not who I was or was not.

The two examples of apologies might seem simplistic, but they illustrate what it looks like to show kindness toward self rather than contempt, thus making reconciliation more important than self-protection. Thankfully for us, God meets us wherever we are and seeks reconciliation. The runaway son was full of self-contempt ("I don't deserve to be called your son"). While feeding the pigs, he convinced himself that his father could no longer love him. He attempted to push away his father's love. But the father's way of love overcame the son's defense mechanism of self-contempt, and the party started.

I am convinced that absolute, unconditional, divine love is kryptonite for self-contempt. God's love calls us back from isolation and into relationship. It is this goodness that begins to turn us toward home.

DISCUSSION QUESTIONS

When you make a mistake, how do you speak to yourself? What are the words and phrases you commonly use to curse yourself?

Have you cursed your own body? If so, why? What do you hold against yourself?

Reflect on a time when you felt shamed by another person. What impact did his or her behavior have on your view of yourself and on your behavior going forward?

Consider the apologies you have received from others, and those you have made to people you have harmed. Where can you identify self-contempt? When has an apology led to true restoration?

Where are you now in your experience of God's welcoming love? What can you do to invite it in until it displaces self-contempt?

CHAPTER FOUR

WRESTLING WITH GOODNESS

And now you'll be telling stories of my coming back
and they won't be false, and they won't be true,
but they'll be real.

MARY OLIVER

It's a thing to see when a boy comes home.

JOHN STEINBECK

When he came to himself, he said, "How many of my father's
hired servants have more than enough bread, but I perish
here with hunger! I will arise and go to my father."

LUKE 15:17-18, ESV

TO HAVE VICTORY over self-contempt and shame, we must
have encounters with genuine love. Only an experience with
authentic love exposes the imitation. As Franciscan priest and
author Richard Rohr states,

> Most of us were taught that God would love us
> if and when we change. In fact, God loves you so
> that you can change. What empowers change, what
> makes you desirous of change, is the experience
> of love. It is that inherent experience of love that
> becomes the engine of change.[1]

The runaway son had already tasted his father's inherent goodness: When he asked for his inheritance, he didn't get the response he probably expected. As pastor and theologian Tim Keller points out in his book *The Prodigal God*, "A traditional Middle Eastern father would be expected to respond to such a request by driving the son out of the family with nothing except physical blows."[2] Besides not physically harming his son, the father also graciously gave his son what he had requested—despite how badly it must have hurt when the son requested what he thought was his due, in effect wishing his father dead.

Yet in spite of this experience of his father's unconditional love, the son knew that his attempt to return to the village was a risky endeavor. It is doubtful the runaway expected his father to receive him back home with open arms. To assume that amount of undeserved favor would have been entirely countercultural.

The son was well aware that his community likely would publicly shame him and banish him from his village for life. This Jewish tradition was called the *kezazah* ceremony, which literally means "cutting-off."[3] Jewish boys would be exiled from their community if they lost their money among strangers, which is exactly what the youngest son had done. Public banishment surely would have followed any attempt to return home. The exclusion ceremony would have included a clay container, filled with nuts and corn, that would have been shattered at the feet of the criminal as a sign that the community was casting him away.[4] To avoid this communal shaming and rejection, the prodigal hatched a plan to request the role not of a son to a father but an apprentice to a craftsman.[5]

Yet the prodigal's father would not receive the son's attempts at payback; instead, he invited him into grace and goodness. This was likely nearly unbearable for the son. He knew he did not deserve the love that was being offered to him, and his self-contempt would have made his father's love almost impossible to comprehend, much less accept. But only by returning to his father's embrace would he encounter a goodness capable of changing his perspective of himself—no longer as a runaway from grace but as a beloved son who was back where he belonged.

Our healing journey is similar. Our self-contempt convinces us we are not worthy of the goodness God offers us, so we try to earn his favor and forgiveness. Another way to say it is we attempt to sabotage unconditional love by making it conditional. If we can earn it somehow, love feels more tolerable. In the Son Realm, we must address our core issues of dignity and worth: *Am I worth loving? Can I return home in the state I am in? Will God embrace me or reject me?* The prodigal son was, in one sense, *full of himself* in the arrogant and demanding way he departed his father's house. But it is equally true to say he was *without himself* when he ran away. He did not know who he was apart from his family or his village, or what type of future he wanted. When he found himself in dire straits in the far country, returning home was all he could think about; yet he could imagine doing so only on his knees.

The problem we encounter in this realm is that our journeys inevitably hit similar roadblocks, where self-contempt and shame are our deepest truths. If we hate ourselves, then why would we choose what is best for us? Why would we return home? Our behavior in the external world mirrors the reality of our internal worlds. If we come to hate what is within, we will choose harmful relationships, addiction, shame, contempt, and other destructive behaviors because we believe, consciously or unconsciously, that this is what we deserve.

To begin transformation in the Son Realm, we must see that holding on to shame, addiction, and self-contempt is an attempt to heal something broken inside ourselves. Yet our actions to mend what is broken are misguided (typical methods are disassociation and escapism), hurt the people we most love, and make our souls only more fragmented. Our resulting desperation exposes our need for God and our need to return to his embrace. Dan Allender, in his book *The Healing Path,* says,

> The healing path must pass through the desert or
> else our healing will be the product of our own will
> and wisdom. It is in the silence of the desert that we
> hear our dependence on noise. It is in the poverty
> of the desert that we see clearly our attachments to
> the trinkets and baubles we cling to for security and
> pleasure. The desert shatters the soul's arrogance and
> leaves body and soul crying out in thirst and hunger.
> In the desert, we trust God or we die.[6]

The son's transformation could not have happened while he was suffering in the pigpen. Only when he dared to return home was he given the opportunity to have his foolishness and shame swallowed up by his father's boundless love.

BEARING GOODNESS

We often resist such love. Not only must the healing path pass through the desert to transform us, but we must also wrestle with our inclination to run from goodness—both God's and, as his image bearers, our own.

I see this flight from goodness when clients first enter my office after they have lost control of their lives and are in the midst of deep heartache. All they know is their dysfunction, so to even dream of different lives feels fanciful and out of reach. Why even try?

I don't see this pattern just in new clients; I also see this play out with clients who, after much psychotherapy and soul work, are nearing a place of healing. They sabotage; they relapse; they have an existential calamity or midlife crisis. The truth is that many people are terrified to get well; they are afraid of their God-given power and glory and unconsciously try to return to their pigpens, to what is most familiar.

Healing can be incredibly uncomfortable. We all say we want it, but the closer we get to it, the greater our propensity to sabotage grace so we won't have to face our fears of losing what we know. Staying in the Son Realm works for us; that's why we stay there. When we encounter the kind of goodness that calls us out of bondage, we are often ambivalent at best.

In John 5:6, Jesus poses a seemingly ridiculous question to a lame man: "Do you want to get well?" (NIV). Jesus' question is not as preposterous as it sounds. He could have gone on: "No, really, sir, do you want to get well? Think about it first before you answer. Your whole life will change, you see. You will no longer be crippled in a world that asks full engagement from whole men. If I heal you, I will call you to live as one transformed by my grace. Are you ready for that?"

When we are confronted with the proposition of healing, we must weigh the cost. Our unhealthy patterns become soul ties that are excruciating to break. Turning toward home and embracing goodness can feel like the end of life as we've known it. But Jesus promises that "whoever would save his life will lose it, but whoever loses his life for my sake will save it" (Luke 9:24, ESV). The only path toward this kind of transformation is a journey into the good heart of the Father.

Like the prodigal, most of us have a difficult time accepting goodness. It makes us feel too vulnerable and potentially exposes core desires, which can be terrifying. Goodness produces hope and desire, which feel entirely too susceptible to heartbreak, so we cling to control because we are convinced that the goodness won't last.

Another way to say this is that goodness ruins us, so we obliterate it before that happens. Let me explain this in more mundane terms. My friend's family owns one of the nicest restaurants in Seattle. Canlis restaurant has been in his family for sixty years. The culinary experience there matches the restaurant's breathtaking views of Lake Union. I feel as if I should close my eyes with each bite so I can try to savor the complexities happening in my mouth: hen egg with seaweed; pickled mushrooms; Peter Canlis prawns with dry vermouth, garlic, and lime-artichoke potatoes; Dungeness crab; nasturtium; or my personal favorite, a Canlis salad. I can't even describe to you the beauty in this salad!

The problem with going to Canlis is that I can't afford it. I save up so I can at least order one or two things off the starter menu at the bar. Still, I feel like a king—even though I have to eat a frozen pizza before I go.

After I eat at Canlis, every other meal for the next week is ruined. Nothing tastes as good. I am mildly disappointed in everything until I can slowly forget about the culinary ecstasy I just experienced. Part of me *wants* to forget about the goodness so I can return to being satisfied with my normal meals.

What if unconsciously we do not want what's best for us because it will ruin the familiar, even if the familiar falls far short of the glory we're created for? We eat the frozen pizza because that is what we can afford, and it's the quickest way to fix our shallow hunger. We don't want what freedom and abundance will cost us and what living into that fullness will require, so we settle for less than what God wants for us. Addiction and contempt provide false comfort and control. As C. S. Lewis so eloquently wrote,

It would seem that Our Lord finds our desires
not too strong, but too weak. We are half-hearted
creatures, fooling about with drink and sex and
ambition when infinite joy is offered us, like an
ignorant child who wants to go on making mud
pies in a slum because he cannot imagine what is
meant by the offer of a holiday at the sea. We are
far too easily pleased.[7]

The prodigal son settles for being hired help because he
knows he does not deserve a seat at his father's table. Similarly,
because we cannot bear goodness well, we settle for less and
sabotage all things hopeful and good that could contradict
what works for our pathology. Tasting goodness is terrifying
because it has the potential to ruin us in the best of ways.
Dr. Allender tells us,

We don't know how to hold pleasure and to allow
the fullness of that pleasure to sweep in and over
and around us. . . . I would love for you to begin
to consider how afraid we really are of delight, how
deeply anxious we are in the presence of delight,
honor, glory.[8]

Most of us find it very difficult to truly take in God's
delight in us and his desire to bless us. When faced with the
offer to dwell in the presence of glory and love and the certain
healing that results, we become terrified of the impending

hope and richness. *Could I really be happy? Might I actually do that for a career? Will I have the intimacy I crave in my marriage? Will I become a better parent to my children?* Being happy can take too much faith. The vulnerability inherent in hope triggers us to hit the eject button. We relapse with internet pornography for the sixth time; we lie about where we went after work; we skip therapy when we know we should go. This is sabotage. Goodness becomes difficult to bear, so we look for easy exits from it.

WRESTLING WITH SABOTAGE

So what do we do with our inclination to sabotage the grace of God? A few years ago I was in California facilitating a story workshop with the Allender Center. There were only a few of us leading the workshop, and it felt like an honor to be part of this elite team facilitating such sacred work. The healing that I was helping guide that day was exhilarating and awe inspiring.

This particular Saturday, I had counseled for nearly ten straight hours. That night I hobbled into my hotel room, joyful and exhausted. I started the shower and crumpled to the bottom of the tub, fatigued and delighted. All of a sudden, I had the urge to look at pornography, even though at this point I had been sober for more than six years. I tried to think of something else and began fighting the craving. But instead of white-knuckling it and just trying harder to disregard what I felt, or shaming my body for its arousal,

I attempted to be kind and to listen to what was going on beneath the surface of my compulsion. *What am I seeking in this very moment?* I asked myself. *Why the desire to relapse now? What feelings am I trying to escape?*

I realized what was happening: I couldn't bear the pure delight I was feeling. I was unconsciously trying to do two things: add to my good feelings through distorted pleasure, and rid myself of the good feelings through the shame of relapsing into an old addiction.

Either of these two classic forms of sabotage would have helped me escape the goodness of being part of the healing journeys of those courageous men and women. After self-reflecting, I was able to embrace the beauty and wholeness of the day. Sabotage did not have the last word. But it takes practice and courage to learn how to bear goodness well.

Sabotage shows up in relationships more than anywhere else. I don't know about you, but when I feel vulnerable in a relationship, I unconsciously revert to a primal survival mode, customarily the behaviors I learned in order to survive my own early childhood trauma. I attack, I villainize others or myself, and I dismiss any feedback I receive. Whatever I can't stand within myself I will attempt to unconsciously annihilate in the other person. As Richard Rohr states, *"If we do not transform our pain, we will most assuredly transmit it,"*[9] and it's commonly transmitted to those who are closest to us.

Sabotage happens when we push away the very love we need to survive. When I was dating Christy and we were deep into working out our relationship issues, she was more mature than me in a lot of ways, and more ready to pursue a lifelong commitment. I knew that what we had was good and that I was falling in love with her. It also petrified me to fully surrender my heart and life to another person. I couldn't fully commit to her, so I broke her heart. I tried to push her away and extinguish the goodness of our relationship because it terrified me. I would not tell her what I was feeling, and I would date other people without telling her.

Part of me didn't want to lose Christy, and part of me didn't want to have her. That was maddening and unfair to her. I knew I wasn't quite the man I pretended to be, so I chose the ease of cowardice over the challenge of integrity. I knew she was a "whole" woman; thus, to be in relationship with her, I needed to be a "whole" man. My thought process at the time was *If I can run away from her, destroying what is splendid in our relationship, the beauty will not expose me for the fraud that I am.*

Goodness and beauty always reveal what is truest in our hearts. So when we are not ready to look deeply in the mirror at our own darkness and inadequacy, we sabotage as an attempt to safeguard ourselves from being exposed. Often, when we first imagine letting goodness in, we create defense mechanisms that protect us from further heartache and trauma. These defenses have helped us survive our greatest traumas; we trust them. Yet they are the same things that contribute to our destruction and isolation. For example, when learning to open ourselves up to romantic relationships again after being deeply betrayed and wounded, it takes courage to be vulnerable and trust someone again. The closer we get to healing, the more our defenses are exposed, and this is terrifying. Our defense mechanisms are not fundamentally bad; the problem is that they remain long after the perceived danger has dissipated. Our walls then end up blocking us from others—keeping us safe from further betrayal and heartache, yes, but also isolated and trapped behind the barriers to love that we ourselves have erected.

In order to move out of the Son Realm, we must surrender, as the prodigal finally did, to the Father's goodness and love.

SURRENDERING TO LOVE

Surrendering to love is a sacred act of opening our hands, loosening control, and trusting in a God that we cannot see. I recall a simple metaphor about surrender that I read when I was a teenager. Imagine love is like a little bird that you hold in your hand. If you grasp it tight, you will surely suffocate the bird, and love will have no chance to flourish. If you hold your hands loosely, with your fingers interlocking, the bird will live but still not be free. Only through fully opening up your hands and setting that bird free will you know if love will return and choose you. It is within this terrifying freedom of surrender that true love is experienced.

I remember the moment I knew that Christy was who I was meant to be with. I was sitting in Dr. Dan Allender's class titled "Marriage and Family," and he was lecturing about the beauty and terror of love and the partner we need in such a treacherous journey toward the heights of heaven and the depths of hell. I immediately felt that divine lump in my throat and a pang in my stomach that only God or diarrhea could produce. *What am I doing?* I thought.

The problem was, Christy and I had broken up. I hadn't spoken to her in more than ten months. Another small problem: I was dating an amazing woman. And though part of me loved her, I was not *in love* with her, because I had given my heart to Christy years before. For me to taste the beauty of true love, I had to pursue Christy despite my fear that my hope and goodness could be thwarted. I finally was ready to completely choose what had scared me most of all: genuine love.

After class I began the painful process of breaking it off with my girlfriend. I wrote Christy a letter naming the new conviction and awareness I had been given and apologizing for how I had feared and failed her. A mutual friend was able to find out her address for me. Despite my fear, I sent the letter via snail mail and waited . . . and waited . . . and waited . . .

I received a letter twenty-nine excruciating days later. Many of Christy's closest friends and family were wary of her giving me another chance after I had broken her heart so profoundly. Yet the beauty of my wife is that she sees things in people that others seldom do. Christy saw in me the man of integrity I was stumbling toward, not the coward I had chosen to be in my relationship with her. We spent the next year working through our issues and navigating very tricky waters before we got engaged to marry.

Because of my courage to step into my fear and surrender to a potentially worrisome amount of goodness, and because of my wife's courage to do the same, we have been able to create such sweetness in our lives. The beauty that our love has created reminds me of the glorious party the father threw for his youngest son. As the prodigal returned home, he, too, surrendered to love and was lavished with his father's unjustifiable, enthusiastic grace. As we drop our defenses and loosen our grips of control, we allow goodness to penetrate and transform our hearts. The Son Realm is about surrendering to a God who knows what's best for us and returning home to our honored seats at the table.

DISCUSSION QUESTIONS

How do you receive good gifts, compliments, and blessing? Do you find it difficult to accept goodness? Why or why not?

What are some ways you have sabotaged the good and beautiful things offered to you?

What defense mechanisms do you still use? How do they work for you?

What stops you from loosening your grip of control and moving into a posture of surrender? What are you afraid of?

How can you practice embracing God's goodness and your own?

PART TWO

STAYING HOME:
THE ENTITLED ELDER BROTHER

- **GOAL:** Justice
- **FELT STRUGGLE:** Entitlement
- **PULL:** Power and Righteousness
- **CORE FEAR:** Exposure
- **RESULT:** Others-Centered Contempt and Judgment
- **WHAT DRIVES US:** Comfort
- **WHAT WE MUST ADDRESS:** Pride and Insecurity

CHAPTER FIVE
DEMANDING OUR DUE

It is easy, when you are young, to believe that what you desire is no less than what you deserve, to assume that if you want something badly enough, it is your God-given right to have it.

JON KRAKAUER

The older son was in the field. When he came near the house, he heard music and dancing. So he called one of the servants and asked him what was going on. "Your brother has come," he replied, "and your father has killed the fattened calf because he has him back safe and sound."
The older brother became angry and refused to go in. So his father went out and pleaded with him. But he answered his father, "Look! All these years I've been slaving for you and never disobeyed your orders. Yet you never gave me even a young goat so I could celebrate with my friends."

LUKE 15:25-29, NIV

LIFELONG FAMILY FRIENDS own more than a thousand acres of land deep in southern Mississippi, which they refer to as "the estate." There isn't a holiday get-together that passes without the family meeting and voting on different issues regarding the property. It gets messy with eight brothers and sisters each having strong opinions and owning an eighth of the massive estate. Some of the siblings have long ago moved out of state and want nothing to do with the discord or the small dividend check that comes every quarter from their inheritance. Others believe their father would never have wanted his children to break relationship over something as petty as property. Yet resentments have grown, angry emails have been written, sides have been taken, and, most of all, relationships have been damaged and probably lost completely.

Sadly, this family's inheritance story is not rare; those involved just have more money at stake than most of us. Greed, envy, jealousy, and entitlement seem to come out in talks of money and inheritance. Each of us has an idea of what is just, what we think we deserve, and what we believe we're entitled to.

I remember my client William, a middle-aged man who had suffered enough trauma for two lifetimes. He had lost his mom to suicide when he was a teenager, and his dad was financially supportive but emotionally absent. Will and his siblings were told to move on from their heartache and get over it. The subtle messages he heard were to be a man, suck it up, and be strong for the rest of the family. Will grew up quickly, lonely and confused, but made a vow to be the best son for his hurting father and his disoriented siblings.

Will is the nicest guy you'll ever meet, but I learned not to trust his niceness. It took me a while to realize why: He agreed with everything I said. No pushback, no disagreement; pretty much just blind acceptance. After a time of this type of interaction, I became quite annoyed and suspicious. I told him that I wished he wouldn't be a yes-man, always agreeing with me. I explained how nervous his compliance made me.

The story of his years of being the obedient elder brother came to the surface. The more he shared, the more I learned: His father still paid Will's rent, his college loans, and all his bills, including for therapy sessions. Will hadn't had a job for the past eight months. After wrecking his car on the way to a therapy session, he said to me, "I'm not worried. My dad will just get me another one."

My jaw nearly touched the ground. I replied, "Did you hear what you just said? You had a pretty large lapse of judgment and wrecked a car that was given to you by your father; yet there will be no consequences for your error, and you just expect your father to get you another one? Do you hear how that sounds? Quite arrogant of you, huh?"

He agreed. We continued to explore why he felt so entitled to his father's wealth, and it came out that he thought his father owed him a great debt because he blatantly neglected William's emotional needs and ignored his years of quiet suffering. William genuinely desired his father's love but most likely would never receive it, so he decided to take everything he *could* get.

Will's sense of entitlement from his teenage years caused him not to live into his age, rendering him unable to keep steady work or follow a unique calling or path in life. As a result, he battled depression and anxiety. Before Will could experience healing and freedom, he was going to have to decide to cut off his father's financial support and begin to choose genuine relationship over security.

In the same way, the elder brother in Jesus' parable felt he deserved to be paid off by his father because of his amount of sacrifice and suffering (his hard work in the fields). As psychologist and professor Dr. Jim Coffield often states, "The level at which you sacrifice is the level to which you feel entitled." I see this dynamic often with those who are stuck in a legalistic mind-set. Because they have seemingly been obedient in following the rules, they believe (consciously or not) that God should reward them.

But in the case of the elder brother, Jewish tradition would have asked more of the elder than the younger. Theologian Brad Young says that in the culture of that time, the older son would have been expected to act as the mediator in the family crisis set in motion by the younger son's demands. "He should tell his father that he will set his brother straight," Young writes. "He should argue with his brother. Instead he does nothing." After his younger brother left town, he might actually have had a financial incentive to do nothing. Dr. Young again points to cultural tradition and, citing Deuteronomy 21:16-17, suggests that in response to the younger brother's request, the father would have had to give his elder son his portion as well.[1] In his book *The Parables: Jewish Tradition and Christian Interpretation*, Young writes, "The elder brother received a double portion, two-thirds of the family's accumulated wealth while the younger brother received only one-third. The elder brother's silence shouts at the first-century audience. He quietly receives his share of the money without involving himself with the broken relationships in his family."[2]

Many times we want the benefits of work minus the suffering, or we want resurrection without crucifixion. Of course, in one sense the elder brother did work hard, but relationally he was a coward; he dodged familial responsibilities that could have caused him emotional turmoil. Yet because he sacrificed much during his time working the estate, he felt justified in kicking his feet up when it came time to do the hard relational work he was supposed to facilitate.

The elder brother enjoyed the benefits of his little brother's rebellion. He got to scapegoat him as the bad and sinful one while resting comfortably in his arrogant self-righteousness. The last thing he would have wanted was for his sibling to return home empty handed and be honored with a celebration. He was convinced that he himself was the loyal one—the committed, dutiful, and faithful son—and if he did receive payment of two-thirds of the family estate, as Young suggests, he certainly wouldn't have wanted to return it. The elder would have wanted to keep his father's wealth, convincing himself that he had earned it.

This posture of expecting God's favor without confronting our obstacles to right relationship with him and others marks many of our restoration journeys. My clients sometimes desperately look to me to repair what is broken inside them. "How do I get well, Andrew? Can you fix me?" Early on in my practice, I would answer those questions with

"Well, there are no easy answers or twelve-step programs; a long and arduous journey is ahead." It was true but not very compelling. For the past few years, I have been trying a different approach. When the client poses the question "What do I need to do to heal?" I now simply say, "You must suffer, bleed, and die."

My clients typically look at me with horror and intrigue. However, despite my propensity for using provocative words to elicit emotional responses, I truly mean it. We cannot taste resurrection until we have drunk deeply from the cup of suffering. The elder brother refused to lean into the suffering that came to him and engage in his family's relational drama. He wanted the gifts of the father without accepting the cost of remaining in relationship.

We all want to get well, until we know the cost. We like the idea of becoming new and whole, until we realize what it will take. We think that God should spare us from suffering because we have lived dedicated lives. Our entitlement inclines us to think that wholeness will (or should) come quickly, painlessly. But the journey through healing change couldn't be more different. As Jesus says in John 16:33, "In the world you *will* have tribulation" (ESV, emphasis added).

Our work is to learn how to let the suffering arise and enrich our lives rather than to resist it. We must not have a sense of entitlement when it comes to our own healing; instead, we must gather the courage to enter into difficult emotional territory, something the elder brother wasn't willing to do. Healing cannot be inherited or caught from someone else; we must take the death-defying pilgrimage of restoration for ourselves. This involves engaging our stories, telling ourselves the truth about our conditions, grieving our suffering, and choosing to break unhealthy patterns in our relationships.

I am reminded of the story Jesus told of the tax collector and the Pharisee:

> He told his next story to some who were complacently
> pleased with themselves over their moral performance
> and looked down their noses at the common people:
> "Two men went up to the Temple to pray, one a
> Pharisee, the other a tax man. The Pharisee posed
> and prayed like this: 'Oh, God, I thank you that I am
> not like other people—robbers, crooks, adulterers, or,
> heaven forbid, like this tax man. I fast twice a week
> and tithe on all my income.'
>
> "Meanwhile the tax man, slumped in the shadows,
> his face in his hands, not daring to look up, said,
> 'God, give mercy. Forgive me, a sinner.'"
>
> Jesus commented, "This tax man, not the other,
> went home made right with God. If you walk
> around with your nose in the air, you're going to
> end up flat on your face, but if you're content to
> be simply yourself, you will become more than
> yourself."
>
> LUKE 18:9-14, MSG

Jesus continually calls us to look at ourselves in the mirror and tell the truth about what we see. Just as it was for the Pharisees, the journey toward humility is difficult. Yet the sooner we can admit to harboring our own inner, entitled elder brother, the sooner we can let go of the sense of entitlement that keeps us isolated from relationship and the very heart of the Father.

CONFRONTING OUR SELF-RIGHTEOUSNESS

The Elder Brother Realm represents our entitlement and also births a fierce self-righteousness. Demanding what we believe we are due pushes us toward a prideful stance that thwarts our ability to love. Novelist Paulo Coelho wrote in *The Alchemist*, "If someone isn't what others want them to be, the others become angry. Everyone seems to have a clear idea of how other people should lead their lives, but none about his or her own."[3] Our harsh judgment of others must be engaged within ourselves in order for healing to progress.

Let's look at Luke 15:29-30 (NIV, emphasis added), where the elder brother interacts with his father:

> Look! All these years I've been *slaving* for you *and never disobeyed your orders.* Yet *you never gave me* even a young goat so I could celebrate with my friends. But when *this son of yours* who has squandered your property with prostitutes comes home, you kill the fattened calf for him!

Do you sense the accusations toward the loving father? The aggressive judgments toward the younger brother? Do you hear what is beneath the elder brother's words? The manipulation, the anger, the righteous indignation, all sprinkled with bits of fact? The younger brother did squander, and he probably was with prostitutes; yet he was treated like royalty. There was plenty of truth to justify the elder brother's resentment and judgment. He was the son who had endured and stayed behind and worked tirelessly. He put his own blood, sweat, and tears into his father's estate. He was proud of what he did and how well he did it. He wanted justice, and the father's grace seemed to offer none. The elder brother wanted to see what was clearly so wrong put right.

We, too, are inclined to put forth evidence to validate our righteousness and convince ourselves that we deserve more from our heavenly Father. The elder brother inside us screams for justice, so we strive for perfection and then feel entitled to receive what we feel we deserve. When others are not working as hard as we think we are, we become callous and justify our resentment. But by judging others from our bloated egos, German pastor and theologian Dietrich Bonhoeffer writes, "we blind ourselves to our own evil and to the grace which others are just as entitled to as we are."[4]

My wife has always had a rich spiritual life. When she was in college, she bought herself a wedding ring to represent being married to God. She spent the next twenty years believing that she was different from other believers, truly the singular bride of Christ. A few years ago, after she lost a close family member in a tragic accident, Christy's spiritual life wavered greatly. In the first sermon she preached after the death, she revealed to the congregation that she had always believed she was too special for God to ever allow such a close family member of hers to pass away. She thought that he would protect her from that sort of pain because she was a preferred and beloved bride. She had believed unconsciously that she was entitled to a life without such heartache and bereavement. She went on to confess that she had judged others who had lost loved ones as somehow not as loved by God as she was.

Everyone was silent as Christy admitted her entitlement and her judgment. "And then," she went on, "I heard the Lord say, 'You are just as special and just as chosen as every other person who has ever lost someone they have loved. You are just as special and just as chosen as the women in Afghanistan who grieve over their children blown up in the streets. You are no different from all whom I call my sons and daughters, my bride.'"

Like Christy, the elder brother and younger brother are equally chosen and special to their father. The faithful and sacrificing sibling is just as chosen and special to the father as the rebellious and unfaithful one. But the elder brother is blind to his sins of entitlement and judgment. He is not willing to sit with his anger, be with his brother, and attempt to understand what his brother's journey was like and what he learned. The elder brother is consumed by his own sense of betrayal. To have a posture of curiosity, the elder brother would have to swallow his pride and come toward his brother with an open heart.

This is what the Kingdom of God looks like: mercy and humility rather than revenge and arrogance. And this Kingdom reality is what drove the elder brother crazy. His father's welcoming posture toward the prodigal was so unfair! To make himself feel better, he took a self-righteous stance. Neuroscience researcher Dr. Alex Korb writes in his book *The Upward Spiral*, "Despite their differences, pride, shame, and guilt all activate similar neural circuits, including the dorsomedial prefrontal cortex, amygdala, insula, and the nucleus accumbens. Interestingly, *pride is the most powerful* of these emotions at triggering activity in these regions"[5] (emphasis added). Like shame and guilt, judgment and pride act powerfully on our brains. But the neurochemical response to judgment and pride is a reward: They literally make our brains feel good!

The elder brother inside us wants justice more than mercy. We feel that if we have been "good," we are entitled to preferential treatment by God. But we cannot manipulate the heart of God. He is not indebted to us; rather, we are indebted to him. In the Elder Brother Realm, we must confront our propensity toward entitlement and pride that leads us to stern judgment.

EXPOSING OUR INSECURITY

The posture of entitlement that leads to judgment is fueled by insecurity. To hide our insecure places, we project contempt

STUMBLING TOWARD WHOLENESS

(others-centered contempt) in order to feel better about our own deficiencies. I will feel better about my insecurities if I can first judge yours. The elder brother's insecurities were evident in his lack of confidence in his father's love for him: He lashed out at his father and complained about not being given a party like his younger brother was receiving. If we are living from the insecure elder brother within ourselves and a conflict arises, we will let fear instead of love rule us.

For me, this issue of insecurity shows up most clearly in my marriage. The irony of our marriage is that my wife gets the very worst and the very best of who I am. The heights of heaven and the depths of hell are bound within one relationship. There are times when my wife will make a basic request: "Would you mind picking up your clothes on the bathroom floor?" or "Would you mind cleaning the kitchen?" or my all-time favorite, "I have my seventh birthday party/baby shower this month, and it's really important I am there. Can I go?"

When I am overwhelmed by my workload or have gone too long without properly caring for my own needs, I can react defensively: "Well, I did take out the trash, take the kids to school, make breakfast . . ." or "You've gone out with your girlfriends four times since I've had a poker night with my buddies." My justifications and resistance can go on and on. I already have my guard up. I'm already looking for a fight, if only unconsciously, because I'm feeling that my wife doesn't appreciate all the hard work I'm doing (even if I didn't clean the kitchen or pick up my clothes on the bathroom floor).

When I feel defensive and reactive, I feel very young,

maybe about twelve years old. This is the tender part within me that my defensiveness attempts to protect. My insecurity comes to the surface as reactivity. Also beneath my knee-jerk reactions is the fear that Christy would prefer to spend another evening with her girlfriends than pursue my heart and spend time with me. But rather than having the courage to be vulnerable with her and say what is really going on with me, many times I do what's easiest.

I actually don't want to be mean to my wife; I like her (most days I really do). So why do I revert to an insecure way of being? The simple answer is, I learned it. The more complex answer is that it continues to work for me. I learned it from my family of origin. Recovering from our parents' divorce without any emotional processing, my siblings and I turned on each other: survival of the fittest, or survival of the cruelest. I developed a sharp wit and a mean bite. This protected my underbelly from the others' aggressions. And still today, if I can hide my insecurity from my wife by being defensive, I won't feel exposed.

This dynamic happens most often in our deepest, most intimate relationships because we know that our partners see right through us; they know our truest selves. I don't want to be exposed by my wife, as she already knows my deepest insecurities, and I'm afraid she will use them against me. (She doesn't.) I choose to protect myself rather than have the courage to be scared in front of her, to be vulnerable with her about my fears of not being enough, of not having what it takes to love her well or be a good father. The irony of this dynamic is that I defend greatest where I most need love. These vulnerable places inside me are the very places that need tenderness and deep care. What I find when I lean into these raw places is that I am actually terrified to be loved well.

One of the greatest fears for an insecure man is exposure of what he most wants to hide and protect. We want to conceal the young, tender places within our souls, thinking that if these places were found out, we would be less likely to be loved.

So how do we stop reenacting an insecure, defensive way of being? First, we must gain self-awareness and continue to enter vulnerability. A new awareness starts by asking ourselves tough questions such as *Who have we become in light of our stories? Where do we feel the most insecure? The most entitled? Why do we judge others so harshly?* When we feel ourselves beginning to defend, we must stop and ask, *What am I defending right now? What am I scared of? Do I trust who I am right now enough to show my heart?*

I have learned that a key to giving up my defenses is to first have gratitude for the way they have saved me and served me. I must bless my story. "Thank you, sharp wit and defensive posture. You kept me safe from harm and injustice. I am now an adult and no longer need you to protect me, as I can now protect myself." When we have gratitude toward our insecurities and defense mechanisms, we can find the strength to release them. This creates a humble posture wherein our entitlement cannot breathe for long.

If we can ground ourselves in what is true (such as my

revealing to my wife my honest, vulnerable feelings of fear and insecurity), we can begin to create new ways of being that are rooted in courage and openness. The more we expose our innermost vulnerabilities in trusting relationship, the more others are drawn to our goodness. When I am brave enough to reveal my insecurities to my wife, she responds with kindness and understanding. She moves toward my wounded places with tenderness and love.

Perhaps the elder brother's core problem was his refusal to be vulnerable about what was beneath his entitlement and resentment. It's possible he was petrified that he was not as loved as his younger brother. He was unable to access love toward his brother and yearn for reconciliation the way his father did. What if instead of judging his brother and resenting his father, the elder brother had recognized vulnerable feelings of anger, sadness, fear, and betrayal; mustered the courage to acknowledge his insecurities and how his various forms of defensiveness (contempt, entitlement, judgment) served to protect him; and then made a conscious choice to let them go, stepping into forgiveness and vulnerability with his brother and father? How might this have changed his relationships and brought reconciliation instead of separation?

How differently things might have played out in the story if the hurting elder brother could have eventually embraced his father's words, "My son, . . . you are always with me, and everything I have is yours" (Luke 15:31, NIV). Even though he still would have felt hurt and angry, maybe those words would have eased his deep fears of not being loved and chosen. He may not have judged his brother so harshly or acted entitled to his father's gracious gift of inheritance. He could have joined the party and entered into the glory of the resurrection.

Consider taking some time right now and locate where you connect with the Elder Brother Realm in regard to your own feelings of entitlement and self-righteousness. What insecurities are beneath these feelings? Are you aware of how your own insecurities affect your relationships? Taking time to engage these questions will help you expose what is inside that needs nurture and care.

DISCUSSION QUESTIONS

What can you do to you allow yourself to be curious about your own propensity toward judgment?

What are some ways you have unjustly projected your feelings of insecurity and self-righteousness onto someone or something? What would it look like for you to take responsibility for your feelings?

Identify some ways you harbor insecurity. How does your insecurity influence the way you judge others?

How can you open yourself to what God wants to reveal to you about your own internal elder brother? What are some practical ways you can combat your insecurity, entitlement, and judgment?

CHAPTER SIX

OWNING OUR CONTEMPT FOR OTHERS

*Each of us must turn inward and destroy in himself all
that he thinks he ought to destroy in others.*

ETTY HILLESUM

*Darkness cannot drive out darkness; only light can do that.
Hate cannot drive out hate; only love can do that.*

MARTIN LUTHER KING JR.

*When this son of yours who has squandered your property with
prostitutes comes home, you kill the fattened calf for him!*

LUKE 15:30, NIV

"LOVE YOUR NEIGHBOR AS YOURSELF" is a command written in
the New American Standard Bible eight times. It is a foundational principle toward which we as followers of Christ must
stumble, and we must sacrifice daily in order to achieve it.
It is important to understand that we cannot truly love our
neighbors until we develop a healthy love of ourselves. The
love of a self-loathing person is love with a lid on, so saddled
with dysfunction that it's nearly impossible to give or receive.

The opposite way to state Jesus' words might be, "Hate
your neighbor as you hate yourself." Self-contempt inevitably
morphs into others-centered contempt. We can't love deeply
from our cores when we hate our cores at the same time.

Just like entitlement, contempt toward others guards

what is really going on inside our hearts and gives us a false sense of control. "It directs our sight away from our deepest longings and deflects the focus from our depravity and need for a Savior to an attack against our own or another's dignity," writes Dan Allender.[1] Or as one of my clients eloquently said, "When faced with intimacy or vulnerability, my internal world goes in search of something to hate in the other in order to avoid the risks of being known. And what better to hate in another than something I already hate in myself? Then I get to be safe—free from the kind of vulnerability that has cost me so much in the past."

As we explored in the previous chapter, vulnerability and intimacy can be terrifying proposals, so we use others-centered contempt to shield ourselves from this risk. The elder brother most likely feels betrayed and abandoned by his younger brother as well as used and unappreciated by his father. He probably is envious of his father's ability to forgive and love more fully than he can. But instead of facing what was inside him and approaching his brother and father with his genuine, vulnerable feelings, he lashes out with contempt for his brother as a way to ricochet his own rage. Theologian Paul Nuechterlein points out, "The elder son's rant about his brother is particularly harsh (verse 30), referring to him as 'this son of yours' instead of 'my brother' and characterizing the squandering of his inheritance 'with prostitutes'—no previous mention of prostitutes by Jesus in narrating the story."[2] The elder brother responds aggressively toward the father and attempts to make his brother's dishonor even worse.

What is the elder brother trying to escape through his others-centered contempt? I would argue that he is trying to cover up his own sin. He is glad that his little brother has been deemed the troublemaker and the black sheep of the family. The younger son returning home will mess with the new-found comfort and wealth the elder "golden child" has come into. As Brad Young points out, the Jewish laws of inheritance state that "the property remains like a trust for the father. He is able to give orders to the servants and maintain limited control over the estate (Luke 15:22-24, 31). The father has divided the inheritance between both sons, but the law of the Mishnah gives him a measure of control over the estate's assets until he dies."[3] When the father throws a huge party to mark his younger son's return, the entire village is invited. The cost of the fattened calf and all the trimmings literally take money from the trust and decrease the elder's inheritance.[4] His contempt for the whole arrangement is palpable.

The reality of others-centered contempt and the sin it obscures is not exclusive to this parable but alive and well in our everyday lives. Some of the most searing violence I have experienced has taken place in my therapy office. I work predominantly with men, many of whom have used their power to intimidate their partners and violence to get their ways. Part of my job is to expose that violence with kindness and strength while also speaking truth into that pattern of abuse. At times this has gone well; other times not so much, and I have even feared for my safety. There is something terrifying about being seen naked and defenseless that brings out the hottest rage.

I remember one family who sought help for their teenage daughter. As the father, mother, and daughter walked into my office, the tension was profound. The mother began speaking of not knowing how to engage their "rebellious" daughter and feeling caught in the middle of a continuous feud between her daughter and husband. I turned to the husband and asked him what he thought the problem was. He snarled venomously, "She is disobedient, has never respected me, and needs to be taught a lesson." The violence beneath his words caught me off guard. He continued, "She has never even liked me. Even as a baby she would not come to me. Something is wrong with her."

I turned and looked at the daughter, who was staring down at the floor. I asked her how she was feeling, hearing this, and she just shook her head, not saying a word.

I don't know if this was the best move (you seldom do in the therapeutic process), but I decided to engage the man's violence head on. I asked, "Sir, when you speak to your daughter, do you normally talk with such an edge to your voice?" He mumbled something in return. I continued with my observation: "I am wondering if it's difficult for her to know that you love her when your tone is so harsh."

I could feel his rage begin to shift from her to me, and I told him so. "Even now I see that your rage has begun to turn in my direction. It is quite intimidating. It's okay, albeit unnerving, because I can handle it, but maybe your daughter cannot, and that is why she does not respond well to your demands for compliance. As I check in now with my body, I feel my own fear in confronting you, like you will make me pay somehow. Yet my bind is that you are also compensating me to have the courage to tell you the truth, despite my fear." This was met with strained silence, so I continued. "I think your daughter does need continued support from a therapist, but so do you, and I am willing to walk beside you as you discover how your contempt is playing out in the story of your family."

At this point the wife's jaw nearly hit the floor, and the daughter's face showed shock and awe as she waited for the nuclear warhead sitting next to her to explode. The man's face was expressionless as he perhaps contemplated punching me or just ending my life right there on the spot. I was hoping he would choose neither option and would have the courage to deeply reflect on the state of his own heart. I hoped he'd see how his contempt for others held intimacy at arm's length, never letting the people he loved most get close. His daughter's rebellion was merely a covert, brilliant scream for love. She was the victim of an aggressive, insecure man and a passive, frightened mother who enabled the abuse to continue. The man's unaddressed pain was being projected onto the most vulnerable member of the family. My job was to get him to own his self-contempt, which had turned into contempt toward his daughter or anyone who confronted him with truth. He did choose to come back to see me a few more times but, sadly, did not continue. I hope and pray that he can address the angry elder brother inside himself and heal his own wounds rather than pass them on to his offspring.

OWNING OUR ANGER

Most of us are angry at something. We are angry at our parents for what we didn't receive as a child; we are angry at what we are not receiving from our partners as adults (or maybe we are angry that we don't have partners at all); we are angry at our boss, our children, ourselves. The elder brother in us rages at all that is not right with the world. If you are not angry at something, I would ask you why. There is much injustice in this world to be angry about. Healthy anger can be a powerful agent of liberation and justice. But maybe you are disconnected from your anger because the proper use of it was never demonstrated well in your family of origin. Or maybe you were taught that anger was bad, even a sin. I would argue that both repressing and indulging anger are hurtful to relationships and unhelpful to the healing process.[5]

I can picture the elder brother indulging his rage, spittle from his mouth flying toward his father's tender face. I can imagine him roaring with aggression, "How dare that son of yours come home after all he put us through, all he has wasted! I want nothing to do with him!" The elder son is angry and has a right to be. His problem here is not with his anger; it's with what he does or doesn't do with it.

The same is true for us. The feeling of anger is just a

feeling, neither good nor bad; it's part of what it is to be human. But we must come into a healthier relationship with our anger so it doesn't turn into contempt toward those we are angry with. Dr. Robert Masters, in his amazing book *To Be a Man*, speaks of skillfully expressing anger. "Well-handled anger, however fiery it might be—or might need to be—does not feel threatening or dangerous, but builds more trust and safety, thereby helping to deepen intimacy."[6] Because anger without contempt or aggression is vulnerable, it actually draws people closer!

So how do we engage our anger well—without indulging it and becoming aggressive and contemptuous, and without repressing it and becoming numb, wooden, and merely "nice"? I wonder what it would have looked like if the elder brother had engaged his anger in a mature way that invited deeper intimacy with his father and brother. Imagine the story reading this way:

> The older brother felt deep love and relief that
> his brother was now home safe. But he also felt
> a deep anger at the betrayal and pain his brother
> had caused. He knew he needed to talk to both his
> father and brother before he felt ready to join the
> celebration.
> His father came out first, and they began to
> talk, taking turns sharing how they felt. The son
> said, "Father, I am feeling so many conflicting
> emotions right now. I love my brother and am glad

he is home safe, but I am also very angry! I am furious at how he made such a poor decision and then just decided to come home like nothing ever happened! And you treat him like royalty when he returns? I have worked so hard here and have stayed so loyal, and I feel deprived that you haven't given me even the smallest of celebrations with my friends."

His father responded, "Son, thank you for telling me how you feel. It is good to know your heart. It makes a lot of sense why you feel such anger. But it is important to remember that we thought your brother was dead, and now he is alive. We must celebrate his resurrection. He will learn valuable lessons of maturity and growth only through our honest and vulnerable love. You must tell your brother all that you are feeling. I will go get him so you can talk to him."

I imagine this mature elder brother speaking to his rebellious brother in a way that honors the complexity of the elder's feelings, that allows anger and love to coexist as he vulnerably tells the truth of his experience. His brother hears the love he has for him and can respect the elder's anger regarding his selfish actions. After the elder brother feels heard, he allows his younger brother to tell his side of the story—his isolation, loneliness, and raw hopelessness. Through hearing each other's stories and maturely expressing what is going on beneath the surface, both brothers are able to walk away feeling heard and understood, which enables them to begin the process of forgiveness and healing.

Even though it seems the elder brother doesn't engage his anger very maturely in this story, at least he doesn't suppress it, which is equally damning. If the elder brother buries his anger or acts as though it didn't exist, it will undoubtedly morph into passive contempt, aggression, or both. Disowned anger will eventually come out sideways. This type of passive-aggressive response is the subtle and dangerous kind expressed by many folks who are "nice" but completely cut off from the truth of their anger. This outward "niceness" leads to disconnection from authentic living and a proclivity to stay in the Elder Brother Realm.

CONFRONTING ENVY

In addition to learning how to engage our anger without aggression, we must confront our inner elder brother's inclination toward envy. The elder brother in the parable envied the younger one, and the best way he knew to sidestep this reality was to have contempt for him.

This has been true for me. I remember my childhood friend Michael. He was a a good-looking, charismatic guy as well as a stellar tri-sport athlete and president of the student body and the Fellowship of Christian Athletes (FCA) at the rival high school across town. I, too, was a multisport athlete and a pretty good-looking guy with my own brand of charm.

I, too, was president of both the FCA and the student body at my school. We were natural rivals.

Except I don't think he looked at me the way I looked at him. His family was intact and owned a successful business in our small town. My family was broken and poor. I used my leadership roles and athletic prowess to prove my worth rather than lean into my God-given gifts. I was an insecure success, and when leading out of insecurity, the glory will not last. I envied Michael's wealth, his beautiful family, his father seeming to care about him, and how he never seemed to suffer the way I did. The elder brother inside me envied him as a way to escape my own pain.

When living in envy, I did not have to reflect on the heartache or brokenness of my own life or family story; rather, I could use my idealized fantasy version of Michael's life to deaden my own longings. As we indulge envy, we hide from truth as a form of escape and utter relief from our fragmented worlds.

The elder brother clearly was envious of the younger one's welcome upon his return, as he says to the father in Luke 15:29, "You never gave me even a young goat so I could celebrate with my friends" (NIV). He wants what the younger brother has (acceptance, love) but is unwilling to ask for it in a healthy way. This envy quickly turns to contempt toward the younger brother and continues to add distance in the siblings' relationship. If we can become aware of our own propensity toward contempt and envy in the Elder Brother Realm, we can then see our own need for both giving and receiving forgiveness, which is key to letting go of our contempt and envy and reconciling the relationships we most long for.

EXTENDING FORGIVENESS

Forgiveness feels like such an easy theme to pick out of this story, yet there is nothing easy about it. I have heard this term casually tossed around so much that it has almost become nauseating. In his marvelous book *Wishful Thinking*, Frederick Buechner says that sometimes familiar quotations are "so familiar you don't hear them."[7] The same is true for religious words like *forgiveness*. Worse, I've seen forgiveness employed as a weapon of shame rather than a tool for freedom. I hear it used to silence those who come into my office looking for healing from their past sexual abuse or from a violent marriage. I hear it from the well-meaning pastor who says, "You need to forgive your father/husband/grandpa and move on with your life." Forgiveness can be used to hush the one who has been sinned against rather than to shatter shackles and set the wounded free.

I believe we should forgive those who have harmed us, of course, but forgiveness is not the first or final response to our exploitation. Before we can forgive from the heart, we must honor our pain and rage against injustice. We must feel our fury at the unfairness, our anger at the innocence lost, and our fierceness that reminds us that we matter and are worth raging over. Forgiveness is not forgetting or neglecting what we feel but fully embracing and exploring it, courageously addressing whatever is there. Like us, forgiveness has a heart-beat; it's not something we do in our heads.

My experience is that forgiveness rises and recedes like the tide. Authentic forgiveness enters my heart and departs just as quickly. Some days I feel I can release my anger toward those who have harmed me, and other days I am just as bruised and livid as ever. I think that's okay. Forgiveness takes us through daunting territory, and no one said it would be an easy journey.

Buechner defines forgiveness this way:

"You have done something unspeakable, and by all rights, I should call it quits between us. Both my pride and my principles demand no less. However, although I make no guarantees that I will be able to forget what you've done, and though we may both carry the scars for life, I refuse to let it stand between us. I still want you for my friend."

To accept forgiveness means to admit that you've done something unspeakable that needs to be forgiven, and thus both parties must swallow the same thing: their pride.[8]

What a difficult undertaking this can be. To swallow pride is sometimes as problematic and painful as swallowing knives. Too often I want to hold on to my pride because it feels like it's the only thing keeping me alive. But I am called to let go, even when it feels like death.

The reason that honoring our true feelings is so important is that when we own our hurt and rage, we can begin to feel our underlying grief, and as we grieve, we learn to surrender. I believe that *surrender* and *forgiveness* are nearly interchangeable terms, and both involve a process. When we can honor what we are feeling without shoving it down or numbing out, we can begin the journey toward surrendering the pain, shame, and contempt inside us and emerge where true forgiveness is possible. This journey of release is the one the elder brother must take to liberate the younger brother— and himself—from the shackles of his contempt.

It is easy to think that the elder brother should have just forgiven the younger one and joined the party, and maybe he did—we don't know the end of the story. But when I reflect on my own propensity to hold a grudge, I don't know if I would have been able to celebrate the prodigal's return. Would you be able to forgive so quickly? Maybe you are more in touch with God's mercy than I am, or maybe you avoid confrontation at all costs and offer a cheap version of forgiveness (an attempt to forgive without engaging your true heart) so as not to rock the boat. Whatever you do with forgiveness, it's important to look closely and reflect honestly on your relationship with it. God calls us to a radical form of forgiveness through the example of his Son, Jesus Christ. Our forgiveness cost Jesus his very life, and for us the call is no different. We must suffer and die in the way we forgive. It will be painful, and it should be.

Now, this hardly seems fair, you may be thinking. Why

does forgiveness have to be painful? Why should the victim experience further suffering in the process of forgiving the violator? It's because if forgiveness is truly about surrender and, as Buechner says, swallowing pride and principle, then it may feel like death. The elder brother might have to swallow his pride like a lump of coal and only reluctantly open his heart to his brother again. But in the process he can open himself to his father's invitation to feel the fullness of his humanity. In doing so he can eventually release his contempt and envy and experience the glory of the celebration. Our Father wants the same for us, and in his embrace we will be comforted.

DISCUSSION QUESTIONS

Historically, what has been your relationship with anger? What about your own anger? Would you consider how you engage anger to be either repressive or indulgent (both missing the mark of healthy anger)? If so, have you considered what another possibility could be?

How has your own unaddressed anger been projected on those around you?

Have there been times when you have stayed in envy as a way to shield yourself from pain or living in truth?

What have you been taught about the concept of forgiveness? How can you move into authentic forgiveness?

CHAPTER SEVEN

ADDRESSING ABANDONMENT AND BETRAYAL

A generous heart is always open, always ready to receive our going and coming. In the midst of such love we need never fear abandonment. This is the most precious gift true love offers— the experience of knowing we always belong.

BELL HOOKS

Ours is a faith that embraces wounds. It's not that it celebrates pain or relishes in it. Nor does our faith ask us to seek out pain or suffering, as if our redemption is tied up with how miserable we can be for Christ. But our faith refuses to gloss over our woundedness with hollow positive thinking. It refuses to ignore that basic tenet of human life. We will hurt.

DAVID HENSON

"My son," the father said, "you are always with me, and everything I have is yours."

LUKE 15:31, NIV

HER FACE IS FIRM. She is listening obediently to the phone held to her ear and answering in short phrases, which is very different from her usual exchanges. I know immediately that she is on the phone with someone in her extended family. They are talking about "business," about land taxes or some such thing, and I can see that she is bearing a lot and saying very little.

My wife is kind, doesn't like to rock the boat, and follows the rules. She is a helper, a people pleaser, and she loves others very deeply. When we travel down South every Christmas to visit her large Catholic family, my wife gets a sizable check from her grandmother. We are ever grateful for this money, but there can be strings attached, which doesn't feel good. These expectations are rarely spoken aloud, but my wife feels subtly indebted because of these gifts and how they keep her bound to her sin of being the stereotypical elder brother (not to worry—she agrees with this assessment).

Christy has always worked hard, has never caused trouble, and has continually done what was expected of her. She developed this way of being the "golden child" as a response to her parents' divorce, which was like an earthquake to the family dynamic. As the third of four kids, she found herself the caretaker and peacemaker. While her siblings responded to the divorce with more typical acting out, such as abusing alcohol and running away from home, Christy responded by doing even better and becoming even more well behaved. She was the "good girl" her parents knew they could always count on.

Unconsciously, Christy adopted this role in an attempt to win her parents' approval and affection. She could not get their attention through running away because her siblings were already doing that, so she made a vow that seemed logical: *I will become the superlative child.* She continued to excel in everything she did—being a star athlete and top student, earning multiple advanced degrees as she got older. She tells me she wants to go back to school and get a medical degree (she already has a doctorate in psychology).

My wife's core fear was being abandoned and unloved for who she really was underneath her veneer of perfectionism. This drove her to make vows that guided her—and sometimes still do—into reenactments of unprocessed trauma. John and Stasi Eldredge say that vows are a "deep-seated agreement with the messages of our wounds."[1] Even though she desperately desired to be loved and pursued by her parents, my wife's vow to be perfect only caused her to be more abandoned and isolated, envied by and disconnected from her siblings, and unable to be honest about her own pain. The latter would have rocked the boat, which went against her vow to be good and not cause her parents trouble. She determined to hold in her pain concerning her parents and siblings and look instead to many members of her extended family and friends to meet her core relational needs.

The problem with Christy's taking on the role of the elder brother, trying to be perfect both then and now, is that it leaves her lonely. The thing her vow pushes her to get—love—is the very thing the vow prevents her from receiving.

The younger brother and the elder brother are no different. They are both seeking to meet the same core need. They want to be loved; they just pursue different means of getting that essential longing met. For many of us, our commitment to the false salvation of doing our duty, being good, or being right leads to loneliness and feelings of abandonment. Did the Pharisees have a deeply intimate relationship with Jesus?

Were they part of Jesus' inner circle? No. Their idea of being "right" or having the perfect doctrine was the very thing Jesus condemned most.

Jesus crafted the elder-brother character specifically for his audience of Jewish leaders and Pharisees. Luke 15:1-4 reads, "The tax collectors and sinners were all drawing near to hear him. And the Pharisees and the scribes grumbled, saying, 'This man receives sinners and eats with them.' So he told them this parable" (ESV). Jesus wanted his stiff-necked, self-righteous hearers to contemplate the arrogance at the heart of pharisaical culture.

The elder brother in us represents our own inner Pharisee. When we are committed to seeking justice over mercy, having correct theology over caring for those we are in disagreement with, then a self-righteous, unyielding posture creates distance in relationships and abandonment for all involved. The elder brother in the parable was *faithful*; he spent every day working with and for his father and never left home as his younger brother had done. He was *consistent and reliable*—his father's cornerstone. Yet the older brother was so committed to being perfect and earning his father's approval that he did not know the glory of being chosen and loved. The elder brother could not access a place of longing for relationship because he had not allowed himself to need compassion and connection.

One of my seminary professors, Dr. Steve Brown, once said, "It is much easier to hug a dirty kid than a stiff one."[2] This speaks to the rigidity of our own inner elder brother.

Even though what we do can be "right," we often miss the love that's in front of us. I think of the godly parents who attend church multiple times a week while their own children are longing for their presence at home. Is it wrong to go to church so frequently? Of course not. But just like anything else, even churchgoing can become an idol and thus become wrong.

All good things can become idols, just like not-so-good things. Although the commitments our inner elder brother makes are often quite virtuous, they can be used to hide from intimacy rather than pursue it. We must be aware when our elder brother, who determines to do what is right, gets in the way of what God wants with and for us in relationships.

HEALING BETRAYAL

Besides protecting ourselves from abandonment, many of us choose to stay in the Elder Brother Realm because of our fear of betrayal. The elder brother is generally considered bad in our reading of the parable. He was greedy, judgmental, insecure, and entitled. But consider the possibility that he was not only irate but also heartbroken by his brother's leaving. Imagine all the years these brothers played together—the experiences they shared. The prodigal's abandonment might have had a profound impact on his elder brother. In fact, the elder son might have felt deeply betrayed by someone he once trusted. It may seem like a stretch from the text, but I would argue that the elder brother's level of contempt could not have been so passionate unless his wounding was great—that is, unless he had lost something he loved.

Also consider what it must have been like for the older brother to watch his sibling break his father's heart. It's possible the elder brother's love for the father is what inspired his rage toward his sibling: "The father is the source of my flourishing, so I will love him jealously such that whoever hurts him hurts me." How hot his indignation must have been toward his brother for making their family vulnerable by disrupting their plans and financial stability. He may have felt justified in treating his brother as poorly as his brother had treated them. Whenever we feel abandoned and betrayed, we tend to lash out rather than sit with the pain of the absence of the one we love.

Of course, it is possible that I am wrong about the elder brother's love for his younger brother. Sibling relationships in Scripture are not typically affectionate and loving. Cain murdered Abel, Isaac was favored over Ishmael, Esau threatened to kill Jacob, Leah and Rachel competed harshly for Jacob's affection, Joseph was nearly killed and sold into slavery by his brothers, Absalom killed his brother Amnon, and so on. I'd say the biblical norm in sibling relationships is conflict, not conviviality. Yet regardless of the elder brother's motives, the father was calling him into deeper relationship with his younger son and himself. He was asking the elder to be authentic with all that he was feeling, including the tension between his love and hate.

God asks nothing less of us. If we reside in the realm of the elder, unaddressed feelings of abandonment and betrayal can have more power over us than we realize. We abandon ourselves with regularity because of our fear, arrogance, and judgment. We must offer unconditional love to our elder brothers just as much as to our runaway sons. We must bring our elder brothers back into relationship with a heavenly Father who has a special place in his heart for those who are abandoned (see Psalm 68:5).

The father longs for his older son to forgive and come join the celebration of his younger son's return. The father has desired only one thing since his son left: for his sons to be united and his family to be together again. The younger son's return is a miracle, and now the father is eager for the reconciliation of his entire family.

The only way this can happen is by the elder brother coming to the table and joining his family with honesty and vulnerability. What if the elder son's encounter with the father is an invitation for the son to process his grief, his anger, his fears? He must confess his hurt, rage, and jealousy so that his heart is soft enough to welcome his younger brother back home. Likewise, confession of our own pain, anger, contempt, and envy must happen before we can be free enough to forgive and to open our hearts to love again.

STUMBLING TOWARD GOD

Each of us is a lovely, complex mess. The church is made of people, which means that the body of Christ is a beautiful mess as well. We are all stumbling toward God, attempting to become more like Christ, and it's not a pretty transformation process. I am reminded of the social activist Dorothy Day, who wrote, "As to the Church, where else shall we go, except to the Bride of Christ, one flesh with Christ? Though she is a harlot at times, she is our Mother."[3]

The elder brother is much like all of us: Within him is a rich glory and goodness that goes hand and hand with his deep depravity. Glory and depravity are always two sides of the same coin, meaning that which makes us glorious also most likely harbors our deepest sin.

For example, since childhood I have been prone to lead. Even when I was a young kid, everyone in our group of boys would listen to me; they would follow my lead, for better or worse. This has continued throughout my life. I am a natural leader. My default is to behave with authority, and consequently people follow. This trait has been key in my journey toward naming my calling, a calling that demands I speak truth into systems of power and take hits from those who are envious of my natural gifting or feel threatened by me. My calling plays well in my therapeutic work with people who are looking to be seen and challenged and are in need of a strong advocate. This is part of my glory.

Yet my gift is also my curse. My propensity to speak truth can make it difficult for me not to be a cynical and critical person. I can quickly see people's darkness and where they are in hiding, and this doesn't make me a welcome guest at dinner parties. I can be standoffish and arrogant. My truth telling can bring life and light into people's lives as well as heartache and destruction. My glory and depravity will be forever conjoined, just like the elder brother's, yet Jesus sees to the heart of my nature and calls me his beloved.

The scandalous message of the gospel is that God loves us despite our self-righteousness, entitlement, and greed and invites us into relationship and resurrection. Transformation begins as we surrender our addiction and entitlement and make our way toward confession and reconciliation. As this happens, we find ourselves moving toward the Father Realm, in which we are at peace with ourselves and those we are in relationship with. It is this realm that we are designed for, yet as we will see, it is the realm we fear the most.

DISCUSSION QUESTIONS

What role has abandonment played in your story? What is your response to this sense of abandonment? Can the elder brother's cover-up of his own heartache teach you something about what you do with yours?

What are your stories of betrayal? How do they shape the contours of your inner world and outer life?

How do your glory and depravity interplay? Have you made peace with this reality? If not, how might you move toward recognizing and accepting this dichotomy?

What resentments are you harboring that you need to be set free from? As the elder brother must come to the table with his family and be honest with his hurts and pain, what must you do to be honest and open your heart?

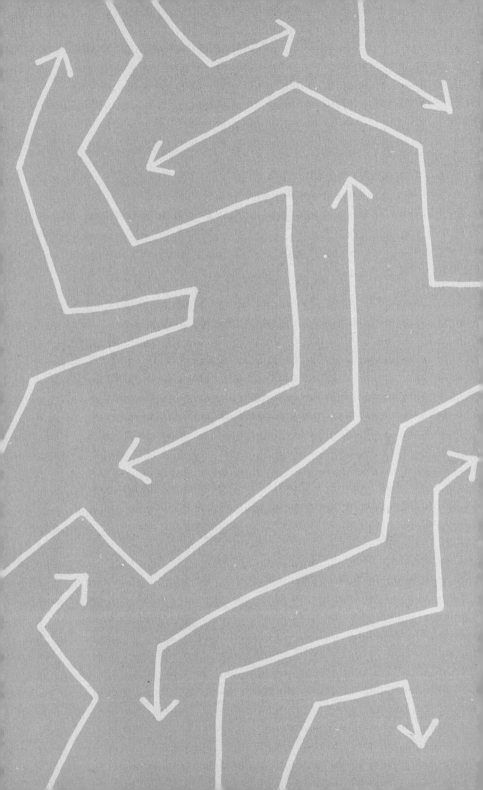

PART THREE

RETURNING HOME:
THE WELCOMING FATHER

- **GOAL:** Restoration and Healing
- **FELT STRUGGLE:** Embracing Grief/Kindness to Self and Others/Surrendering Control
- **PULL:** Kindness
- **CORE FEAR:** Rejection
- **RESULT:** Celebration and Resurrection
- **WHAT DRIVES US:** Willingness to Risk
- **WHAT WE MUST ADDRESS:** Issues of Control

CHAPTER EIGHT

GRIEVING OUR WOUNDS

*Sadness does not sink a person; it is the energy a person
spends trying to avoid sadness that does that.*

BARBARA BROWN TAYLOR

*I don't believe that grief passes away. It has its time and
place forever. More time is added to it; it becomes a story
within a story. But grief and griever alike endure.*

WENDELL BERRY

*While he was still a long way off, his father saw him coming.
Filled with love and compassion, he ran to his son, embraced
him, and kissed him. . . . "Quick! Bring the finest robe in the
house and put it on him. Get a ring for his finger and sandals
for his feet. And kill the calf we have been fattening. We must
celebrate with a feast, for this son of mine was dead and has
now returned to life. He was lost, but now he is found."*

LUKE 15:20, 22-24, NLT

THE FATHER'S HEART IS A GRIEVING HEART. This may sound odd,
as the Scripture tells us the father was "filled with love and
compassion" (Luke 15:20, NLT). Yet we must realize that love
and compassion are not incompatible with grief. They are
actually a prerequisite. Because the father loves his son so
deeply, the father must grieve to the same level of love.

To understand the magnitude of the father's grief, we
must revisit the weight of the son's betrayal. Verse 12 is

commonly understood as the father's property being divided: "The younger of them said to his father, 'Father, give me the share of the estate that falls to me.' So he divided his wealth between them." But theologian Paul Nuechterlein points out that the Greek word referring to the father's property, *ousia* (a word used only twice in the entire New Testament, here in verses 12 and 13), means "being" or "existence." The Greek word *bios* in verses 12 and 30 refers to the father's wealth but is translated as "life." We are accustomed to reading this familiar text with the assumption that literal wealth or property is being divided (and ultimately squandered). But if we read the passage through the lens of life and existence, it might sound more like this:

> The younger of them said to his father, "Father, give me the share of [your] *existence* that will belong to me." So he divided his *life* between them. A few days later the younger son gathered all he had and traveled to a distant country, and there he squandered his *existence* in dissolute living.[1]

This interpretation brings the depth of the father's grief into bold relief. He is not only faced with grieving the potential literal *thánatos* (death) of his runaway son but is also called to forfeit his own life, his very existence and being.

What might this mean in literal terms? The father opens his heart to wounding and transgression. He is willing to let his heart break in response to his son's rebellion. He relinquishes control, risks rejection, and embraces brokenness.

The father models a posture of vulnerability and courage made possible by his willingness to fully enter suffering and loss. With this posture, the father also creates the possibility for restoration to occur in the son's life. Vulnerability and courage are contagious and can be caught by those we love if we can first boldly blaze the trail.

Grief and joy are related. The reason the father was able to receive his son back into relationship and celebrate him so wildly was that he was willing to grieve his son's death deeply: "This son of mine was dead" (verse 24). To the father, the runaway son had passed away in the most tragic fashion, on his own in a distant land where the father was powerless to help in any way. The father had a funeral in his heart for his youngest boy: He entered the depths of heartache and despair.

In light of the agony of loss, doesn't the fierceness of the father's love make more sense? There is no way the father could love or celebrate life with such abandon unless he had plunged to that same level of affliction.

If we want to grow beyond the escapist impulse of the prodigal son and the resentful legalism of the elder son, we'll need to face our grief. Once we do, we'll find ourselves in the Father Realm, where true healing and reconciliation await. As the thirteenth-century poet Rumi said, "The wailing of broken hearts is the doorway to God." Grief plays an essential role in our lives, carving within us the capacity for love, joy, and glory. We must permit grief to take residence in us and bless its occupation in our lives. The deeper we grieve, the higher we can rise on the tide of love and the more able we will be to experience the Father's joy.

ENTERING OUR GRIEF

To move toward joy, we must have the courage to grieve what has been broken in our lives. This requires a willingness to grieve our stories of loss, to mourn with courage at what treasure has been taken or what dream has not come to fruition. Was your childhood innocence lost as a result of sexual abuse? Was your heart broken by your father's violence? What did your mother's passivity and manipulation create in you as an adult? To let pain matter is to honor your story; to honor your story is to honor yourself.

My friend Cathy Loerzel, director of the Allender Center, speaks about grief and joy as though they were on a continuum, with the deepest grief on one end and the greatest joy on the other. If you're like me, you more often than not choose to stay in the middle of the continuum, where you are not vulnerable to heartache and harm. Moving toward grief feels too risky because of the potential for heartbreak, and moving toward joy feels too risky because of the potential for letdown.

But the capacity for joy that transcends death is proportional to the depth at which we are willing to grieve. If we have grieved our losses only superficially, we may miss the fullness of joy when the time for gladness comes.

What if we weep to the point that we feel near death, as though we were walking through life with no skin on? People's words and actions pierce us as we hobble along, not knowing if we can endure one more blow. Loneliness and exhaustion become our only food. Our stomachs are tying knots around those knots. That is a depth of anguish we barely survive. But when we are willing to walk through it, we come out the other side with a much greater capacity for joy.

It's important to note that we need not go searching for grief in an effort to experience joy; that's not how authentic grief works. When we live with open hearts, tragedy and heartache will find us whether we like it or not. The question is not whether grief will arrive but whether we will have the courage to become intimate with it when it does.

Because grief requires us to acknowledge and surrender to our throbbing, it is easy to have contempt for our pain and resist grieving it. We all have deep caves of sadness within our hearts, but few of us choose to take the courageous expeditions into ourselves to face and address these shadowy caverns in redemptive ways. It is easier to play it safe, to escape or get addicted (the Son Realm), or get furious or entitled (the Elder Brother Realm). But the Father invites us into a realm of lament and joy as the redemptive response to suffering. It is within the abyss of heartache that we find the hope of resurrection, and avoiding pain denies us the very liberation we so desperately desire.

Extreme grief has come only twice in my life, and I barely lived to tell the stories. During those seasons of darkness,

I wrestled much with grief. Facing such heartache never comes easy. I imagine this process as much like the account in Genesis 32:24-30 of Jacob wrestling with God. We wrestle with grief until we are exhausted, and it marks us. We never truly get over it; we learn to go through life with a forever ache.

Grief will come to us all. We don't choose grief; it chooses us. We must choose what we do with grief when it inevitably arrives. When heartbreak has come to my own life, I have honored it well at times, and other times I have run. When running from the pain, I tried different modes of coping, including a smorgasbord of addictions, shame, and contempt tactics toward myself and others. I tried zoning out in front of the TV and playing endless games of Scrabble and chess (okay, Madden NFL Mobile, too) on my iPhone. Then my self-contempt would fire up, and I would criticize myself for wasting so much time. If making myself the villain didn't work (it never does), I would just project my contempt onto others in an effort to lessen the pain of my heartache. All these strategies numbed me for a short time, but none actually mended what was broken inside.

Grief always exposes who we are. It's a magnifying glass that enlarges our greatest failings, our fullest glory, and who we are meant to be. We must surrender, as the father did, to what makes us most human: this capacity to feel, smell, see, taste, and hear in our bodies the depth of loss when we have put our love on the line and wound up empty handed and bewildered. At times, it feels as if we were being flogged with shards of glass. The weight of grief is heavy on our chests, as though we were buried under the earth.

We can assume that the father in this story was not always mature with his grief and his ability to enter such deep love and compassion. The father was a son before he was a wise father; he went through a learning/maturing process that his sons had yet to experience. This is our journey of maturation as well: We enter the Father Realm by making peace with grief so we, too, can have the courage to love.

In grief we are faced with the inevitable decision of addressing our pain through mourning or opting for ways to escape it. We sometimes make an unconscious vow to disconnect, to love halfheartedly, never going all in again. The drawback to these kinds of vows is that grief and love, as with grief and joy, are intertwined. As Episcopal priest and author Barbara Brown Taylor so wisely said, "Sadness does not sink a person; it is the energy a person spends trying to avoid sadness that does that."[2]

Grief serves as a shovel for the soul: It digs, mines, and excavates painfully, at times violently. But deep love enters those very same spaces. If we never allow ourselves to feel the pain of loss and betrayal, we will not feel the fullness of love. No one speaks this truth more poignantly than C. S. Lewis:

To love at all is to be vulnerable. Love anything, and your heart will certainly be wrung and possibly be broken. If you want to make sure of keeping it intact, you must give your heart to no one, not even

to an animal. Wrap it carefully round with hobbies
and little luxuries; avoid all entanglements; lock it
up safe in the casket or coffin of your selfishness.
But in that casket—safe, dark, motionless, airless—
it will change. It will not be broken; it will become
unbreakable, impenetrable, irredeemable.[3]

The father's epic love for his lost son is shown in the
way he runs toward him, abandoning all propriety. Middle
Eastern fathers are not supposed to run; within Jewish culture, this behavior would be considered not only odd but also
shameful. He would have needed to tie his tunic around his
torso so he wouldn't trip, which would expose his bare legs.[4]
The father thus demonstrated that love is more powerful
than shame and contempt. The father's heart loves wildly
because it embraces vulnerability.

The Father Realm always calls us to live in the great para-
doxical tension between love and heartache, glory and pain.
Another example of this joy-and-pain paradox is found in
Acts 7:55. As a deacon named Stephen faced the Sanhedrin's
fury, he "looked up to heaven and saw the glory of God"
(NIV). When he announced this, the Sanhedrin dragged
him away to be stoned. On the precipice of a most grue-
some death, the glory/joy of God was upon him. Stephen
had the courage to enter death and therefore experienced
resurrection.

Tragedy and joy are conjoined. The apostle Paul reminds
us in Romans 8:17 that "we share in his sufferings in order

that we may also share in his glory" (NIV). The entire Gospel of Luke is filled with this idea of tragedy and glory intertwined. Dr. James Coffield writes,

> The biblical gospel of Luke includes stories of the disenfranchised: the leper, the paralytic, the infirm woman. Luke's stories invite his readers to see Christ as the transformer and healer. Luke even begins the grand story of glory in a place that many would consider shameful: a stable with shepherds. God's great story of glory is teeming with stories of the poor, the ill, the neglected, the scorned, but His presence turns the lowly into the exalted. As believers, our stories will be woven together and end in glory.[5]

This idea of turning suffering into glory is the essence of the good news of the gospel, yet the father and sons could not share in the glory of restored relationship without being willing to suffer heartache and grief. Grief and glory are always bound together in a peculiar dance: Where one shows up, the other will always be near. To taste glory in the midst of heartache, we must follow our Savior's example by facing the brutality of the Crucifixion.

The German philosopher Friedrich Nietzsche once said, "Of all that is written, I love only that which one writes with one's own blood."[6] When authors write, poets speak, painters paint, and musicians compose, you know immediately whether they are bringing their entire souls to their projects or are holding something back. The most beautiful works of art are ones that have been suffered for. There is no difference between this and entering your own grief work as an artisan of the soul. The journey will be full of agony, but beauty will rise from your tomb as sure as Christ himself has risen.

The beginning step of arriving at grief's doorstep is Good Friday. This is the darkest of days, when God's face turns from his Son's and Jesus cries out, "'*Eli, Eli, lema sabachthani?*' (which means 'My God, my God, why have you forsaken me?'" (Matthew 27:46, NIV). Good Friday invites us into the anguish and devastation of our own crosses, when we allow ourselves to know the texture of our own agony rather than try to escape it.

Then comes Holy Saturday, when we must taste the obscenity of death and be willing to sit with the unknown darkness alongside the sense of futility and powerlessness. We must continue to mourn and feel the pain that comes with losing someone or something precious.

Finally—yes, finally—comes Resurrection Sunday. We savor the wonders of our rebirth. We are humbled, exhausted, and relieved as we celebrate the wonder of a holy miracle. When we are in Friday, we can't see Saturday, and when we are in the gloom of Saturday, we don't know if Sunday will ever come. Yet when it does, we are full of goodness and joy and love, even as we never lose sight of the fallen world in which we live. We are called to live in the tension of all three days, moving in and out of each and living honestly and courageously in the tension of both grief and joy.

Grief has been with us the entire time. Why resist what is already true? We live in a fallen, broken world. If you live on this earth long enough, you will taste the sour stench of death. If you haven't suffered immense loss or betrayal, you will. So how do you want to die? Do you want a slow, suicidal death from cowardly denial of your own heartache, or a bold, noble death from courageously facing it? You will be dead either way, so how do you want to go out? I would far rather die with courage than hide behind denial.

If you open your heart and surrender your life to God, you will feel the depth of what it means to be fully human. It is only fitting to acknowledge what you already know intuitively to be true. It will feel like death because, in one sense, facing your deepest grief *is* death.

The temptation will be to try to resist your crucifixion. It is understandable if you are afraid to face your own death— Jesus was. In the garden of Gethsemane, he said, "Father, if it is possible, let this cup pass from Me" (Matthew 26:39). Jesus was "deeply grieved, to the point of death" (verse 38), looking for any way out of the agony that was to come. But he knew who he was and the liberation he was meant to bring. He was "obedient unto death" (Philippians 2:8, KJV) and feasted on resurrection.

In the Father Realm, we must allow our hearts to break and then have the courage to love ourselves and others despite the broken places. Though our choices to face our own death stories will not bring the possibility of salvation for an entire world, they will help set others free and must be fought for.

WELCOMING SILENCE

Inviting grief requires us to not only embrace our pain but also equally welcome silence. As the younger son leaves the father, the father experiences an anguish of absence and is forced to face the silence of himself. This vicious departure most likely requires the father to take inventory of who he wants to be and how he would like to father in the future. The father is willing to sit with the uncomfortable silence of his own ache, which enables him to receive the son so radically when he returns, as well as to call the elder brother to the party. Loss has a self-reflective quality about it. Being present with the stillness of our grief tills the soil for us to hear the "still small voice" (1 Kings 19:12, KJV) of our God, calling us into reconciled relationship.

In this current season of my life, I have experienced the least amount of silence. In other seasons, I could hike in the tranquility of the mountains for hours. I would reflect and write, pray, and dream of the future, uninterrupted. Now I have two kids under age four, and our house is very small (but somehow still has a large mortgage). Both my wife and I feel we are going insane most days. I have given up naming what new bodily fluid I am cleaning up or wondering if the stench of that poopy diaper is still in my clothes as I go to work. With the hustle of the big city, schoolwork (my wife and I are on the ten-year track to finish our degrees), run-ning our business, kid craziness, and of course writing on the importance of stillness, my life is a holy mess more often than not. With all the chaos and noise, I sometimes feel so divided and detached from myself and God. But the beauty of the gospel and the splendor of our pursuit of God means that no matter how hectic our lives or crazy our mental states, we can be still and know God (see Psalm 46:10). He is always available, even when we are not.

Luke 15 also contains two other parables that Jesus told, one about a lost coin and one about a lost sheep. These sto-ries depict a God who is a fierce pursuer of what has gone missing. God breaks with tradition to unearth whatever is lost, and that includes you and me.

Stillness can be the doorway into richness and oneness with our Father. The other day my wife was able to watch the kids and encouraged me to go write for a few hours. I drove to the Cascade mountain range, about an hour out-side Seattle, to my favorite little coffee shop. I wrote there for a couple of hours and then felt the need to go for a walk in the woods. I found a quaint place by the river, took my shoes off, read, breathed deeply, and attempted to sleep. It was glo-rious. I pulled my computer out of my backpack, not know-ing what I wanted to say, and wrote. My soul flew. I felt God's presence. The openness and beauty of the location released a part of my humanity that at times the commotion of the city had subdued. I won't tell you what I wrote, but it ended up being one of my favorite sections of this book.

Welcoming stillness is vital to reconnecting with the Father of compassion and truth inside us. I know this is much easier to write about than to achieve, yet the Father's voice is alive in us all! This voice must be fought for and fostered. The poet Rumi once penned, "This silence, this moment, every moment, if it's genuinely inside you, brings what you need. . . . Sit quietly, and listen for a voice that will say, 'Be more silent.' Die and be quiet. Quietness is the surest sign that you've died. Your old life was a frantic running from silence. Move outside the tangle of fear-thinking. Live in silence."[7]

The sacred act of choosing stillness is one way to get in touch with that still small voice within you. How can you be more intentional about your spiritual discipline of stillness? Do you need to get a babysitter and take yourself on a date to slow down and reconnect with you? Do you need to write? Be near water? In the forest? Even just walk around the block? What do you need in order to make this silence a reality today? Listen. God will tell you what and how you most need to take care of yourself. God desperately wants to care for you and delights in doing so.

INVITING OTHERS ALONG

After we have entered grief and welcomed stillness into our bones, we must finally invite others into our most wounded places. Proverbs 17:17 says that "a brother is born for a time of adversity" (NIV). We are meant to have friends who can sit with us in our pain without offering trite answers and easy solutions—friends who will weep and wonder alongside us, such as what is requested in this call for accompaniment:

> *Please don't give me answers; though that is what I say,*
>   *that is not what I long for in this chest of broken*
>   *pieces.*
> *I do not want your sympathy, your pat Bible verses, or*
>   *your lofty promises of prayer. No, I want something*
>   *much more sinister than that.*
> *I ask you to suffer, to take my nails of my grief and drive*
>   *them into yourself.*
> *I ask you to be silent, shut your mouth, and open your*
>   *hands. Don't say you understand.*
> *Just touch me.*
> *Will you hold my hand? Though it's cold and bony, will*
>   *you embrace me tightly?*
> *Can you wail as I wail, curse as I curse, pray as I pray?*
> *I don't want to be fixed; I want to be known.*
> *I want your presence kneeling by my bed, feeling useless,*
>   *powerless, helpless. Yes, for then, for then, you will*
>   *understand a small part of me that few have had*
>   *the courage to know.*
> *I recognize this will cost you greatly, but deep down*
>   *I will learn my worth from the measure of your*
>   *sacrifice.*

I wrote this poem during a dark season of anguish and yearning. Even noble-hearted people with good intentions

STUMBLING TOWARD WHOLENESS

can be careless with a fragile, inconsolable heart. Nevertheless, we must have the courage to invite our community into our broken places.

I remember a time of great grief in college when I needed someone to help carry my broken heart. I went through a painful breakup and could not hold it together anymore. As I wept and lamented bitterly on the single bed in my dorm room, I heard the door crack open quietly. Not even bothering to see who entered, I felt a hand on my back a few seconds later. Not a word was spoken; there was just a hand laid gently upon me. It could very well have been the hand of God, and to me it was.

Eventually, as my misty eyes cleared, I found it to be the hand of my friend Greg. Even though I did not overtly ask him to show up for me in my agony, my posture of broken-ness and grief was an invitation for him to come. True grief is an open door for good, courageous people to walk through. Greg loved me enough that day to enter. Though I could have felt shame for letting him see me in that condition, I knew his love and kindness toward me was to be trusted, so I allowed his care to mend my fragmented heart.

After minutes that felt like hours, he got up and walked toward the foot of my bed. He slowly and carefully began to remove photos from a shrine to my girlfriend that I had created. Without knowing it, Greg was caring for my heart in a divine way. I had never received that type of care from a friend. His courage to love me and grieve alongside me brought me back to wholeness. Others knew of my heartache but were too frightened to approach me for fear of saying something wrong or because they felt the futility of trying to help. Yet it was Greg's mere presence that I needed the most. He just showed up, and in doing so he showed me the father-heart of God.

The vulnerability of this scene was twofold: Greg was vulnerable in the way he cared for me, not knowing if I would receive his gift or not, and I was vulnerable in allowing him into my pain. This is the essence of life-giving relationship—when grief is honored by both the one who is caring and the one being cared for.

Whether it's the father's sorrow as the son betrays him, the brokenness of the youngest son as he returns home, or the elder brother's conviction of his self-righteousness, we all need people to be with us during our seasons of despair. Those of us who remain alone in our grief can feel more and more alienated from the people around us. It is so important to lean into our loneliness and seek the communion that our aching hearts deserve. If we can give ourselves permission to grieve, then daring, devoted friends will show up.

If those people do not show up in your time of need, ask yourself if you are allowing your brokenness to be seen or only breaking in isolation. How vulnerable are you willing to be? If you have not been courageous up to this point, it is possible you have not attracted gutsy, trustworthy people into your circle of friends. As you fully enter your grief and begin to heal, you will draw people into relationship with you who are or have been on a similar path. But you may have to go looking for them. Maybe you need to attend a new church, an Alcoholics Anonymous meeting, or a therapy group. Don't stop seeking others to join you on this journey. There are courageous sojourners who are willing to enter both the hell and heaven of life. If you stumble forward long enough and reach out, you will find them.

DISCUSSION QUESTIONS

Where are you on the continuum between grief and joy? What wounds do you still need to face within your own life in order to increase your capacity for joy?

Have you allowed yourself to weep to the point of exhaustion? If not, what is your resistance to feeling your grief?

Are you aware of what glory will come when you enter the suffering of your story? Write down a description of it or create a piece of art that depicts what you hope to find.

Take fifteen minutes to find a quiet place by yourself, take a walk in the woods, or sit by the ocean. In this stillness, what do you hear? Don't talk—just listen. What is God whispering to you? What stops you from engaging with silence? What are you so terrified to discover? Ask God to grant you courage to face what is within.

Are you aware of those who are with you on your grief journey? What action will you take to invite those trusted few along?

CHAPTER NINE

ENGAGING KINDNESS

I am so tired of waiting,
Aren't you,
For the world to become good
And beautiful and kind?

LANGSTON HUGHES

Be pitiful [kind], for every man is fighting a hard battle.

IAN MACLAREN

The older brother became angry and refused to go in.
So his father went out and pleaded with him.

LUKE 15:28, NIV

ONLY AFTER A DECADE of walking through my own healing process and having the sacred privilege of walking alongside hundreds of people through theirs has the power of God's kindness to transform become tangible to me. Shame and contempt are not motivators for change; rather, they are hammers that drive sin deeper into our souls. Proverbs 11:17 says, "Your kindness will reward you, but your cruelty will destroy you" (NLT). Until the beginning of my own therapeutic work, I didn't even know that self-contempt was a problem. Now the way I treat myself on a daily basis has changed, as has my understanding of how God's kindness and blessing lead us all to the freedom we long for.

The apostle Paul says in Romans 2:4 that God's kindness "leads us into a radical life-change" (MSG). The greatest motivator for my own transformation has been the kindness and blessing of God. I continue to learn how to live into what I believe is most true of me.

Therapist Sam Jolman writes, "No one changes in a continuous straight upward path. Change always involves stumbling and failing and just outright blowing it. And therefore, change requires immense kindness and grace. If we have no compassion for ourselves, we simply cannot muster the energy needed to get back up and keep going."[1] Kindness to self is a lost art in Christendom, yet without it we become stuck in the early part of the restoration journey. Kindness is the grease of God to get our transformation moving. Kindness gives us the ability to press on even in the darkest of times.

I remember when I began my journey toward kindness. The power was captured in a grainy, faded picture of me and my father on a beach somewhere in Florida. I was probably five or six; he was slender, strong, and good looking. His arms were reaching toward me as I ran away in absolute joy of being chased by my father. The picture sat on my desk for a few years. Many days it was just too painful to look at. I longed to believe that the laughter on our faces was real—that my father loved me. Did this picture capture the pinnacle of the relationship between my father and me? Did it depict his longing to be in relationship with me? Or was this one of the only moments when father and son would ever truly be father and son?

The picture haunted me. I would get lost in this iconic image of what could have been, what should have been, what was not, and what never will be.

For some reason, I kept looking for hope in the photo, as if God were calling me back into the pain to address some unfinished business. I felt as though the picture would help me discover answers to my present-day struggles of loving myself. I kept dreaming that if only I would look deep enough, six-year-old Andrew would hear my adult voice whispering, *Everything is going to be okay. Never give up. You will become a great man, Andrew. You do not have to prove anything. You are enough. You are loved. I am so proud of you.*

Over the years, I have been learning to speak this way to myself, to bless myself with kindness. I bless my young, hurting boy who needed to be fathered. I give myself a love and affirmation that I never received. I have discovered that I can father the fragments of myself that remained so orphaned up to that point, nurse the broken pieces, and wait patiently for them to heal.

This is the experience of the Father Realm: parenting our younger selves through whatever means we can find. Engagement with this transforming kindness comes through confrontation, play, and blessing.

KINDNESS THROUGH CONFRONTATION

The father's confrontation with his elder son is deeply rooted in love and the kindest of acts. As the elder brother spews venom toward his father, the father does not cower but speaks of life and resurrection in the face of aggression and hatred. "We had to celebrate and be glad, because this brother of yours was dead and is alive again" (Luke 15:32, NIV). The father's confrontation is not intended to shame or harm his son for his lack of grace toward his brother; rather, the father models a confrontational kindness for the sake of love and redemption. Just as Jesus did in flipping tables in the Temple (see Matthew 21:12-13), the father's fierce love here is captured in how he fights for the elder's restoration. He desperately wants the elder brother to join the party and taste the joy of unconditional love.

It is important to remember that kindness is not mere niceness. Kindness is not for the faint of heart nor the chronic people pleaser. Holy kindness is not a (with my best Southern accent) "Well, bless your little heart" type of sweetness. In the Father Realm, we need to confront ourselves and those we journey alongside with deep strength and tenderness. The father in the parable models this for us all.

We see this same type of kindness through confrontation in 2 Samuel 12, when the Lord sends Nathan to confront David about his immorality. Nathan says to David, "Why have you despised the word of the LORD by doing evil in His sight? You have struck down Uriah the Hittite with the sword, have taken his wife to be your wife, and have killed him with the sword of the sons of Ammon'" (verse 9). Yet David knows Nathan loves him (see 2 Samuel 7), or he never would have been able to receive Nathan's words. David would have had him killed. Nathan's confrontation through kindness is what opens David's heart to hearing the difficult truths of his depravity. David immediately repents and owns his failures, saying, "I have sinned against the LORD" (12:13). David first knows that Nathan loves him, and that is why his heart is open toward his kindness of difficult truth telling.

Love precedes kindness. Without love, we cannot be kind. The elder son knew the father loved him, and that is probably why he felt safe enough to rage at him. We also don't know the ending to this parable. Did the elder brother join the party after all? Maybe the father's kind confrontation brought the elder brother the clarity he needed in order to change his attitude and behavior. We have no idea. But I do know we can hear kindness in confrontation only when it is rooted in deep care for the other. This type of kindness leads to repentance.

Confrontation alone is never enough to evoke change but must be rooted in deep love. Kindness through confrontation is something I use nearly daily in my therapy practice. Confronting people's impenetrable walls takes a balance of present strength and persistent tenderness. I am reminded of the metaphor of a home. As therapists (and all those walking beside the wounded), we can come to our clients' homes, stand on their doorsteps, and knock lightly, but we cannot barge in and break the doors down, as that would be traumatizing and invasive to those we are trying to help. But we are to stay near, on the porch, waiting close by until we become trusted confidants and receive invitations to enter into their holy spaces in the innermost sacred rooms of vulnerability.

KINDNESS THROUGH PLAY

Kindness is intended to lead to the full restoration of one's playful heart. I believe that this holy playfulness is at least in part what Jesus was referring to in Matthew 19:14: "The Kingdom of Heaven belongs to those who are like these children" (NLT). For us to be kind to ourselves along our journeys and upon returning home, we must be able to play well.

Play is a profound part of our resurrection process, yet it's one of the most difficult things for adults to do, especially men. The type of play I am referring to is not the dissociative type of play, such as playing World of Warcraft more than eighty hours a week. That type of play can be addictive and the same type of escapism that we are trying to extinguish. The holy play I am referring to causes us to be more present and more restored after engaging.

Dissociative play leaves us more drained because we are escaping true life rather than entering into it. If I have a few hours of free time for myself and spend that time playing online chess, watching Netflix, and eating bonbons, I will not feel restored afterward but actually more exhausted. Kindness through play restores the soul. The prodigal is drawn to escapist play, the elder brother can't even imagine what it would mean to be playful, and the father is free enough in the resurrected life to live playfully.

Authentic play is one of the most vulnerable activities we can participate in. Young men are often taught not to feel, that showing emotion reflects weakness. These damaging messages are reaffirmed over and over in male culture, and by the time young boys grow up to be men, there can be a hardness that is difficult to penetrate, and thus healthy play is no longer part of life. This message to men couldn't be more false, as we know that vulnerability takes much more strength than violence. Somehow we have come to think that God wants only our seriousness and devotion; but play takes courage. To live out of our playful hearts is to experience the fullness of our intimacy with God. It is in the play that we let our guards down and become most open to what he has in mind for us.

I remember one year coming home from college on break, when I woke up around noon and entered the bathroom. I stripped off my boxers to get in the shower, and just short of stepping in, I heard something or someone say, *Play, Andrew, play.* I hesitated, trying to understand what I'd just heard, but then it became clear. I heard God telling me to enter into a sacred kindness that echoed Jesus' words in Matthew 18:3: "Unless you change and become like little children, you will never enter the kingdom of heaven" (NIV). So I did. I started running a bath. I searched around the bathroom vanity and found an old bag of green plastic army men. These army men turned out to be my doorway into the Kingdom of God. I set up an elaborate battle around the perimeter of the entire tub, smiling ear to ear. I sat in that tub for more than an hour, laughing and smiling nearly the entire time. That experience of play was so holy that I still remember it fifteen years later.

That day I honored God through my willingness to look

foolish, even to myself. I pushed away the inclination to mock myself and was able to enter into a divine experience of kindness. An enormous inhibitor to our intimacy with God in play is our own sense of shame and association of play with folly. I tasted his kindness through this sacred act of play, and it changed me.

When we trust God's intimate love and care, we can let go and enjoy the abandonment of play. Are you willing to look foolish in order to enter into holy kindness? Are you able to receive kindness through play? How do you play, and how does it change you? These are questions to ponder as you enter more deeply into the kindness of the Father Realm.

KINDNESS THROUGH BLESSING

One of the ways we enter kindness is through blessing. We must choose to bless ourselves as the Father does. We have seen in studying self-contempt that the evil one is in the business of cursing (he is the father of lies in John 8:44 and the thief and killer in John 10:10). Evil does not want kindness and blessing to enter your life and does not want God's voice to be in you. Be prepared to hear lies and intimidation as you journey in kindness through blessing. As Romans 8:1 states, "There is now no condemnation for those who are in Christ," and we must resist evil's pull to condemn ourselves.

The Father Realm is where we are called to bless what has been cursed, which includes those things that have been cursed within us and even those things within us that we ourselves have cursed. The act of blessing is not just positive self-talk but also an affirmation of God's handiwork. You are beauty, you are good; and if that is not how you feel about yourself, you must look at what is blocking you from agreeing with God's view of you.

By naming your beauty and goodness, you are not in any way discounting your sinfulness and failures. Quite the contrary. By knowing your goodness, you can look more honestly at the dark side that is a part of you but no longer defines you. By blessing the inherent goodness of your creation, you are better equipped to adequately grieve your sin and experience joy where joy is called for. How do you speak to yourself? Does your language line up with God's? Remembering "there is now no condemnation," the voice of God's blessing should become your own voice.

I remember a time that I clearly heard God's voice in my own life. I was in my early twenties and had fallen madly in infatuation with a young woman. She was instrumental in unconsciously rescuing me from my family of origin and allowed me to feel special and important. Sadly, participating in the idolatry of another creates an infatuating and devouring type of love that never lasts very long and leaves both people small, hungry, and only partly human. My junior year of college, we finally called it off once and for all, and I was devastated.

Whenever you participate in idolatry and your "god" is taken away, you have nothing left to worship. You lose your sense of identity, you question your personhood, and you are left frantically trying to find your place in the world. I spent many days and nights on the phone with my mentor Jim Coffield, trying to make sense of it all. *Why now? Why not forever? Why does it have to hurt so badly? Where is God?* Jim was gracious and kind as he allowed me to wrestle with questions and unwanted answers.

One late spring day I was telling him of my loss of direction and meaning, not knowing what to do with my life. Summer was coming, and all my previous plans involved "her." Jim asked, "Have you thought about spending the summer in Florida?"

"What would I do there?" I replied.

"You could live with me and my family." He said this with certainty and without hesitation.

"Live with you?" I asked. I felt relief and terror at the same time. "Uh, let me think about it for a few days and get back to you."

I actually did not need to *think* about it at all; I needed to *feel* about it. My body told me what I needed right away: to be loved and cared for by an older, wiser man who would hold my broken heart. Yet I also needed to feel the terror. Why was I so afraid? I didn't know until I called Jim back a couple of days later.

"Have you thought about my offer?" he asked.

"I have," I replied. "I still don't know." And then almost as if my lips were moving without my permission, I said clearly and firmly, "What if you don't love me anymore?"

I was immediately shocked and ashamed at my candor

and lack of nuance. I scrambled inside to recover from the desire and longing that had seeped through my words. "I mean, if I move down there and something happens, that could hurt our relationship."

Jim sat silent for what felt like an hour (it was probably three seconds) and then uttered words I have never forgotten: "Andrew, I made up my mind about you a long time ago. There is nothing you can do to change my love for you."

My heart immediately relaxed, and my anxiety dissolved. I knew I was supposed to live in the Coffields' spare bedroom that summer and recover while embracing the awkward exercise of being delighted in by someone who loved me with God's kindness. Jim showed me the unconditional blessing of a good father, the true blessing of God. He moved toward me when inside I felt there was nothing good I could bring to the table. Through Jim's love, I began to know God's kindness and came to believe that I was someone worthy of love.

Henri Nouwen wrote that the Father's "true voice of love is a very soft and gentle voice speaking to me in the most hidden places of my being."[2] The God who knows our depravity and is intimately acquainted with the shadow places of our souls still runs toward us, just as the father ran toward his prodigal son. When this provocative grace is offered, will we embrace it for ourselves?

The father's blessing to his son is God's kindness that leads to our redemption. It is the voice that gives life, not death—the voice that has no tone of accusation or curse but instead blessing and the highest nobility. The father does not deny the darkness of what the son has done or the pain he has caused; he fully knows the sin but still chooses to run toward his beloved child. The father chooses to bless what the son has cursed. In spite of doubt, he bestows his finest blessings. Despite his grieving heart, he assumes a brave posture of hope. He allows himself to feel delight despite the heartache that hope sometimes brings.

The same is true for our own journeys of homecoming. Just as the father did not humiliate the son, we will not be humiliated as we attempt to make the brave decision to open ourselves to healing change.

RESISTANCE TO KINDNESS

As we taste the father's kind, transformative blessing, we must be prepared for resistance to spring up within ourselves. With hope often comes trepidation and dread. The goodness is almost too much to bear, so we hold blessing loosely, fearing the heartache that will come if the blessing is snatched away. But there is no hope without risk and no healing without hope.

Dr. Dan Allender has written extensively about the ambivalent relationship with kindness, most recently in his book *Healing the Wounded Heart*. He describes sexual abuse victims' tendencies to make war with kindness: "Because 91 percent of abusers are known to their victim, it is highly likely the abuser used kindness and sensitive reading of the victim to create access and trust. Grooming ruins the childlike desire to trust. A kind person will be read with great suspicion."[3] Any betrayal of trust, whether sexual abuse or even benign neglect, can set up a dangerous bias; if someone is caring, there may be a treacherous agenda behind his or her compassionate facade.

The problem is that the very kindness the victim of abuse comes to distrust is the same kindness that God uses to woo his or her weary heart to wholeness and transformation. Do you see the bind? Evil's plot is to steal the kindness of God that is meant to heal the wounded heart. Evil does not want us to be restored and will stop at nothing to thwart God's grace in our lives.

We can see these dynamics at play whether we have experienced sexual abuse or not. How do our own ambivalent relationships with kindness block our access to God's kindness? This is a great time to be curious about your own story on why you resist kindness toward yourself.

Ambivalence is a normal response to this conversation regarding kindness to self, but we must not stay in that place. Prayerfully seek answers as to why you are resistant to God's kindness. Is there a damaging theology that you grew up with holding you back? The teaching that God is out to get you? Or that he is more like Santa Claus, making his list and checking it twice to see who's been naughty or nice? Or is Jesus' death on the cross enough for you, too, and you are truly forgiven and clean—then, now, and forevermore?

Do not let discomfort and heartache distract you from the sanctified undertaking of receiving and practicing kindness. Experiencing kindness means entering pain and grief and accepting it as part of the journey toward transformation.

Kindness is real and sorrow is real, and we must make room for both, not necessarily following sorrow until it leads to kindness. (In fact, per the apostle Paul, it's God's *kindness* that leads to repentance, not repentance as a stand-in for sorrow that leads to kindness.) Kindness and sorrow are forever connected, but when we enter the kindness of the Father within ourselves, we begin to taste the glory of a resurrected self.

DISCUSSION QUESTIONS

What does it mean for you to be kind to yourself? Is this a concept you have considered as necessary for your spiritual growth?

How have you encountered kindness in the midst of confrontation? What has this taught you about how God receives you in spite of your sin?

Have you attempted to bless the child orphaned within you? How has this looked?

Describe a time when you engaged kindness through play. If you have not experienced this, how might God be calling you to do so?

In what ways have you been resistant to God's kindness?

CHAPTER TEN

EMBRACING RESURRECTION

*Most of us were taught that God would love us if and when
we change. In fact, God loves you so that you can change.
What empowers change, what makes you desirous of change,
is the experience of love. It is that inherent experience
of love that becomes the engine of change.*

RICHARD ROHR

*Quick! Bring the finest robe in the house and put it on
him. Get a ring for his finger and sandals for his feet. And
kill the calf we have been fattening. We must celebrate
with a feast, for this son of mine was dead and has now
returned to life. He was lost, but now he is found.*

LUKE 15:22-24, NLT

RESURRECTION MEANS you have triumphed over death. This
does not mean you will not suffer again, but it does mean you
will suffer differently. Living in a fallen world, you will be
marked by heartache, but honoring and entering that heartache will produce perseverance, character (see Romans 5:3-4),
and ultimately hope and homecoming.

The father survived death when his son demanded his
portion of the estate; therefore, he was able to enter the
sacred act of celebration with gusto. He called the servants to
bring his son a robe, a symbol of a high priest. He sent them
to retrieve what was most likely a family signet ring, which

would give the son freedom to do business in the village. The father also gave the redeemed son sandals that signified that he was truly home. Finally, he killed the fattened calf and threw the largest party the village had ever seen to mark the resurrection of his lost son.

The resurrection party is for those who have suffered immense heartache and are willing to show their scars. You have survived whatever tragedy has come your way, and you lived to tell the story. And what a stellar tale you have to tell.

The father's covering of his son is not the masking of truth. It's an acknowledgment of a deeper truth: the truth of his sonship against the lie that his prodigality gave life to. Though the prodigal's scars are covered, the scars—and stories—still remain. Resurrection isn't a reward; it's a grace.

As we prepare to enter the sacrament of celebration, we must be prepared for a dark resistance. The father knew that his friends would mock him and think he was a fool to "waste" the finest on a boy who had betrayed his family so shamelessly. Yet the potential of social mockery held no power over the father. He rejects the Jewish custom of *kezazah*, a ritual of public banishment and humiliation (see chapter 4). Instead he says yes to love for the sake of reconciliation and rebirth.

All goodness comes under attack by evil, and celebration is no different. A restoration party mocks evil's attempt to annihilate what is beautiful. Where goodness is enjoyed, evil makes all effort to take root. So the elder son tries to taint the festivities. But the father reiterates, "This son of mine was dead and has come to life again" (Luke 15:24). He has no choice but to celebrate.

COMING TO THE PARTY

When I learned that the book you hold in your hands would be contracted, I was ecstatic—a lifelong dream was coming to fruition! My wife and I decided to celebrate with a three-day getaway to a fancy resort in Nevada. She and I had never been separated from our kids overnight, and it had been more than four years since we had been anywhere alone for an extended period of time. Christy's mom would fly in from Louisiana and take over the childcare duties so we could be fully present on our trip. Our excitement was palpable. We even discussed the possibility of conceiving our fourth child while on vacation!

I awoke the morning of our trip with some unpleasant anxiety and aggravation in my belly, so I went on a walk and did some breathing exercises. I had a few clients that morning, and with each session, my anxiety began to produce nausea and dizziness. By the time I started my last session at noon, I could barely sit still without feeling as if I were going to vomit.

My client had driven a long way to meet with me, and I felt that I needed to see him. About thirty minutes into our session, I was thinking more about my nausea than about him, so I informed him I would have to end the session due to my illness. My client understood and was gracious, so I immediately hobbled to bed and lay down. My head began to swirl, my body screaming with rebellion against itself.

Over the next twenty-four hours, I experienced an intense headache, a pulsating stomach, and a horrible sore throat. I spiked a fever while simultaneously feeling chills, and at one point I was literally sweating at the same time my teeth were chattering. I chalked it up to a twenty-four-hour flu and felt a little better the next day. Though weak, I was alive, and we decided to fly out on Sunday morning since I was at least walking.

We got on and off the plane without incident, but as we entered the beautiful hotel, I mentioned to Christy that my feet were incredibly sore and it felt like I had some cuts on my hands. She immediately exclaimed, "You have got to be kidding me! You have hand, foot, and mouth disease!"

My first thought was, *No way. We are on vacation!* But our daughter had suffered with this disease the week before. Could it be? Adults rarely contract this wicked rash, but when we got to our room, I examined myself more closely and, sure enough, I saw sores between my fingers and on my toes and heels. And my sore throat was beginning to intensify. The next day, red, itchy bumps covered my hands and feet, and my throat was nearly closed with infection.

One of our first outings was to the pharmacy, where I loaded up on medicine, cream, and sore-throat spray. For the next two days of what was supposed to be a vacation, I was a miserable, itchy mess. I lay in our bed, medicated and covered in white cream. I took an oatmeal bath and went through three bottles of sore-throat spray! My wife could not even touch me for fear of contracting the disease. It was madness! This was supposed to be a celebration, yet it felt more like my funeral.

When I look back on this story, I can't help but wonder if our attempt to enter celebration and resurrection was blocked by a dark kingdom. It would be easy to be mad at myself for the money wasted and say how foolish it was to even try to celebrate my accomplishment. Yet when I consider that I had garnered the courage to immerse myself in the glory of fulfilled hopes, the oddity of my freakish disease makes more sense. Evil is always against new life! Any movement toward celebration will bring on attack from the one who hates resurrection.

The temptation is to play it safe—to not enter resurrection, or at least not party too hard for fear of inciting dark forces. Yet there is nothing left to fear after you have faced down the enemy who tries to thwart resurrection. When you have already journeyed through the "valley of the shadow of death, [you will] fear no evil" (Psalm 23:4). You know that it can no longer intimidate you.

Although I am disappointed that my one vacation of the year was ruined, I know I will be back. I will not let evil have the last laugh. We are planning to return to that same hotel in the spring, and we will celebrate again.

What needs to happen for us to enter fully into the resurrected life characterized by celebration? Why was the father so predisposed to partying while his two sons were not? These answers are found in owning and engaging truth, remembering that God is truth and that the more we live in truth, the more we experience God.

OWNING OUR TRUTH

To enter the Resurrection in the Father Realm, we must choose to live in truth. It means bringing what is hidden into the light, exchanging the inauthentic for the real, unearthing the truths that have been underground for years. The father chooses to live in truth by naming who the youngest son truly is, not branding him for what he has done.

Yet the truth is often difficult to accept. At times it feels that the price of living into truth outweighs the expense of fabrication. I remember Craig, a client who would not tell his wife about his early infidelities some twenty-five years earlier in their marriage. "We are finally in a good spot," he said, and he felt that disclosing mistakes made when he was young might cause him to lose the woman he was now fully committed to. I told him that as I have grown and matured in my faith, I have found the opposite to be true. Living a hidden life always costs far more than living authentically—maybe not in the short term, but in the long tenure of life.

The courage it takes to face ourselves as we are and to tell the truth about what we see is worth significantly more than the heartache that will come of it. Now, I am not saying we must disclose everything in descriptive detail, as that could bring unnecessary pain to those we love. But I am saying we can no longer hide and that masking the shadow parts of ourselves does not lead to a resurrection life but a dead one.

If Craig tells the truth of his betrayal to his wife, he very well may lose her. But what does he lose if he doesn't? Because of his secrets, the very essence of intimacy with her is stolen. Truth is at the core of all deep and genuine connection. Without resurrection truth breathing new life into our relationships, intimacy becomes stagnant and ultimately begins to perish. If Craig chooses to remain silent and hidden, his marriage will surely die: Even if he stays married, intimacy will not survive. When truth is avoided, the intimacy we seek—which is built on trust—will slowly decay, and more and more emotional detachment will create a distance that ensures the withering, if not the termination, of our intimate relationships.

To tell the truth to his wife would feel like a death to Craig. It very well might mean the loss of his marriage. But it is equally true to say that it might be the only way to save it. Truth eventually births new life, even if it initially looks like ruin. Craig chose to continue to keep secrets from his wife and ended up quitting therapy. He just wasn't ready to let go of what brought him so much safety and pleasure, but the cost will be high, and the fall will be painful.

Many religious environments sell perfection as a form of redemption. This lie—that if you obey all the rules, believe harder, and are dutiful enough, faithful enough, you will be able to attain perfect communion with God—manufactures a church culture that, unconsciously or not, encourages hiding under the guise of spiritual "maturity."

I saw this dynamic play out in the college I attended. This particular institution had a "spiritual points" system: If you went to daily chapel services, church on Sundays, and prayer meetings and on-campus Bible studies during the week, you could earn the points that were required each semester. My forty spiritual points didn't quite add up to the required three hundred, and I nearly flunked out before leaving of my own accord. Some eight years after leaving that school, my New Testament professor was caught cross dressing, and my Hebrew professor had had an affair with his son's friend. I don't tell you this to somehow celebrate their pain or even judge their actions but to say that superficial standards of perfection have no actual relation to personal piety or spiritual maturity. If we have no safe places to bring our real struggles, doubts, and heartache, we are likely to stray further from the truth and deeper underground with our pain. I see this stark reality most clearly in the lives of clergy.

A few years ago, the Barna Group launched a nationwide study on pornography called "The Porn Phenomenon." It reports that "most pastors (57%) and youth pastors (64%) admit they have struggled with porn, either currently or in the past."[1] Why? I think it's because pastors and clergy have few people to be completely authentic with. Pastoring can be one of the loneliest professions on the planet. Some churches praise the lone-wolf, faultless image of pastor and push suffering clergy underground with their battles. This creates a duality that if lived with long enough actually causes many to become who they never thought they would be. The report goes on to cite that "87% of pastors who use porn feel a great sense of shame about it."[2] This unaddressed shame sets the stage for living a dual life, which is what ultimately took away my own father.

My father was a minister, a lawyer, and a vice president of a conservative Christian college. He was also attracted to men, and this played out in sexually addictive behavior. His secret festered underground and drove him to feel shame and act out rather than forge truly intimate relationships. My father hid—from everyone. In an attempt to avoid losing everything (his wife and kids, his career, the respect of his peers), he disappeared. The more his secret life became normative, the greater the detachment became between his inner and outer worlds. He became less present, more engrossed in his hobbies, and less interested in spending time with my mother and my siblings and me. His inability to live in truth created an impossible divide that didn't allow him to fully father my siblings and me in any significant ways.

It is impossible to live disconnected from self for very long in committed relationship; something has to break. As my father's dishonesty and sexual addiction became greater, his depression and anxiety worsened, along with his prescription-drug and alcohol dependence. Whatever he could find to bring relief he reached for, attempting to numb his pain and run from the truth.

For my father to live in truth would have required him to be honest about his life, despite the great cost. He would have lost so much in the moment, but in the long run he would have gained abundantly more. First of all, he would have gained his own freedom from the chains of secrets kept. He might have garnered self-respect that was unflappable because it grew out of integrity. If my father had chosen to live in truth and not hide, he may have been able to reenter intimacy with his children and wife and also not struggle with such isolation, loneliness, and despair. As psychiatrist and author M. Scott Peck wrote, "Mental health is an ongoing process of dedication to reality at all costs."[3] Mental health and living in truth are closely linked. When one chooses to live duplicitously, self-contempt fuses within one's identity. At the core of my father, he knew he was a fraud, and he treated himself accordingly until there was little of him left for real relationship.

Eventually, all truth gets birthed, somehow, someway, and my father's secret life was exposed. The fallout was cosmic. He lost everything and never fully recovered. Shame and self-contempt are still daily struggles, and I pray that he will love and forgive himself, as God has already done.

The legacy of hiding from truth continued in my family long after my father was gone. Hiding from truth becomes learned and must be unlearned. It took us years to be honest about our family's story and not let evil have the last word on who we are. In many ways we are still learning how to be truly authentic. It's not easy; actually, it's normally messier than I'd like. But there is a freedom to living in the truth that is greater than the discomfort. The beautiful part of God's story is that resurrection brings fresh life, and legacies of death can become celebrations of new birth.

Truth always leads to some type of death that blazes a trail of liberation, and it is worth every drop of blood shed along that painful path toward freedom. When we live in truth, we defeat the roots of addiction, shame, self-contempt, and the full arsenal that evil uses to "steal and kill and destroy" (John 10:10). My father is and was a good man; there is a deep innate glory in him that he never came to know. My love and longing for him are still rich and tangible, even though he and I have had little relationship my entire life. My desire for him to love me and pursue me will forever be present.

ENGAGING THE TRUTH

Truth can feel like a terrifying monster. The beast comes knocking on our door, hungry and ready to devour; he haunts and taunts our every move. Our response is to bar the door, nailing pieces of wood across the entrance, triple-bolting it, even pushing furniture up to the entry to block the colossus from overtaking us. After the door looks secure, we run into the corner and cower with a variety of weapons in hand. Yet in the face of this posture of fear and timidity, the monster will never leave; its presence will become only more powerful. The more we attempt to hide from its presence, the more authority we give it.

What if we engaged the scary truth differently? What if we invited through the door what we fear most? What if we confronted what is most true, yet equally most terrifying, about ourselves? *Why are you here?* we might ask. *What can I do for you?* Can we listen with inquisitiveness to the behemoths that most haunt us? We must if we are to be free of our fears.

Does your monster have a face? A tone to its voice? After the conversation, you can lead the monster back to the door, reassuring it that if it needs anything else, it can come back for another conversation. But you must also set clear boundaries so the monster can never rule you by its tactics of fear and intimidation again. Cowardice can be a cruel master. Reclaiming your power over the monsters that haunt you is vital to stepping into the transformation the Father Realm invites you into.

What is the reward for living in truth? It is as simple and as complex as access to the Most High. God is truth. Our engagement with truth is at the core of knowing him. All liberation is rooted in he who guides us there. What if each time we courageously entered the truth of our stories we were drawn into perfect, intimate communion with our Creator? We must look at authenticity through this celestial lens, knowing that wholeness cannot coexist with what remains hidden within ourselves. It is not the escapist or legalistic lies we have entered into that ultimately define us, but the Father who pursues us and names us his sons and daughters.

What are practical ways that can help you stay tethered to the resurrected life so you are better able to resist the evil one's enticements into prodigality or resentment? What does it practically look like to enter into the resurrection phase of the Father Realm? Resurrection means new life, so what are you bringing life to? Where in your life is the smell of new birth? Where are you stepping into beauty? It could mean finally sitting down to write that poem that has been on the tip of your tongue, making time to write that book you have always said you would write, or picking up your guitar again or your tennis racket. Whatever it looks like for you, the Father is committed to bringing and sustaining life, and stepping into the Father Realm means bringing truth to lies, light where there is darkness, and life to death.

LOOSENING OUR GRIPS

It is strange to say hello and goodbye to someone who has been such a defining character in my own story and yet a character I know so little of. A few phone calls a year has been about the extent of my relationship with my father, mostly discussing his latest body ailments or the failures of the Tampa Bay Buccaneers.

Yet now I am finding myself longing for those shallow conversations. Our last conversation a few months ago was like talking to a cardboard box with his caricature drawn on the side. He was on the phone but not in his own body. Eight years ago my father was diagnosed with frontal-lobe dementia. The average patient with this disease lives only six to eight years from onset. The Mayo Clinic notes that some people with this condition "undergo dramatic changes in their personality and become socially inappropriate, impulsive or emotionally indifferent, while others lose the ability to use language."[4]

I have lost what little of my father I had left. His one-word, emotionless answers are zombie-like, void of anything I recognize as truly human. My father has never known who I am, but he is dying. I need to say hello; I need to say goodbye.

I bought tickets for my family to go to Florida for a few days to be with him. He had never met my kids, and I didn't know exactly why it was so important to me that they meet him now. "He won't remember it anyway," my brother proclaimed. Yet I didn't think visiting him was for his sake but rather for my own. It felt important that my father and my family should meet, that I should bless my father and whisper my final goodbye. I yearned for some formal ending to this long chapter—a resolution, a completion, an acknowledgment of the heartache of my past and a testament to the goodness of my future. I felt the need to both bless and wail. I needed to just say thank you for the life he had given me and weep his loss in his presence. I needed to grieve beside him, even if he was unable to also do so. I needed to grieve not only his upcoming death but also his life, to loosen my grip on what was not and what will never be.

When I walked into the nursing home, I nearly bumped into a man I hardly recognized. Between sleep and wake, the frail man looked up and said, "Andrew?"

"Dad!" With a few brown jagged teeth and eyes that looked like mine, he smiled. I was jubilant. He remembered who I was; he remembered I was his son!

As I looked at him, the years of my contempt melted and kindness swept over my heart. I hadn't felt this compassion toward him since before he left us, some twenty-five years ago. I softened at the sight of his feeble, fragmented body. His legs were bloodied and bandaged, his body nearly immobile. It had been six years since I had last seen my father, and those years had not been kind to him. He had lost nearly a hundred pounds—not the weight loss that looks like rejuvenation and new life but the much scarier kind that looks like death and bones. His face looked sunken and ready for somewhere else.

As I caught my breath, we engaged in conversation. I told him that Christy and the kids were outside in the car and ready to meet him. He came in and out of lucidity, somehow remembering the grouper sandwich that I had promised to bring him when I'd talked to him a few days before. I told him I would be right back and went to get Christy and the kids. As I stepped outside the door, I began to tremble. My eyes filled, and I could not contain my sorrow. Christy held me while my three-year-old son, Wilder, not used to seeing his dad's tears, asked, "What's wrong, Dad? Why are you crying?"

"Son, it's just hard to see my dad so sick," I responded.

I gathered myself and led my beautiful family into my dad's sad, hollow home. He smiled as I introduced them. I took pictures. He was half there, but today that was enough for me. I am glad my kids got to at least meet half of him. He interacted with them a few times, rolling up Play-Doh and tossing it to them, laughing a bit. Seeing a few moments of delight was enough. My kids were jewels, just excited to be in a new place. Eighteen-month-old Selah waved to all the other elderly folks as Wilder created a clay model of the solar system on the couch (the kid's a genius).

Christy asked if there was anything we could bring my dad from the store besides a grouper sandwich, a Snickers bar, plain Ruffles chips, and a Diet Coke. For his brain to be so nearly gone, he was remarkably sharp in knowing what he wanted. We said our goodbyes when he looked ready for us to leave, and I told him we would return with his treats tomorrow. Before I departed, I looked him in the eyes and told him I loved him. Something shifted in his eyes, as if he had suddenly come back to life. It was like those three words had real power. They unlocked his stuck brain. He stared back at me with an intensity and certainty, saying, "I love you too, Son." No hesitation or confusion, just assurance. I believed him, deeply, and walked out the door. I wept in a way I had not in years. So much built-up grief, covered by years of animosity, poured out of me. My contempt had blocked my desire for my father, but now I could not hold my longing in. I allowed love and compassion for my father to win. This is what it means to surrender unto resurrection.

It wasn't a conscious decision, but it was a courageous one. I did not want to go down to Florida to visit my father, but I knew deeply that I needed to. I felt God calling me toward a bravery that made me uncomfortable. I loosened my grip on the past, and my heart toward my father surrendered to love. This is what healing looks like, this is what resurrection tastes like: The war stops inside our bones, and we become more comfortable with peace than with struggle.

Ted Loder, author of *Guerrillas of Grace: Prayers for the Battle*, pens a stunning prayer on the power of surrender. My hope is that in light of the glory of the Resurrection, we can surrender unto God the Father's love inside us and pray Loder's prayer, asking God to "loosen our grips."

> *Loosen my grip*
> *on myself*
> *that I may experience the freedom of a fool*
> *who knows that to believe*
> *is to see kingdoms, find power, sense glory.*[5]

BECOMING A NEW CREATION

When we are able to step into the Father Realm and into our core goodness, we are able to celebrate and party with a wild hilarity that few understand. This is the resurrected life we were created for. Freedom and surrender are not normal, so do not be surprised if others cannot comprehend. This is what 2 Corinthians 5:17 means when it says that each of us is "a new creation. The old has passed away; behold, the new has come" (ESV). God is the Author of new life and new stories that we get to live.

In this resurrected life, we are not without heartache, but we are living into the ache in a new way. We are not striving toward some unreachable perfection but making peace with both our darkness and our light, knowing that God blesses all of us so we have the courage to do the same.

A metaphor that helps me understand this process of healing transformation is that of the caterpillar. The hungry caterpillar fills up by eating leaves and continues to grow and shed its skins. The caterpillar eventually stops eating, finds a comfortable leaf, turns upside down, and begins to spin itself inside a cocoon, a process called apoptosis. During this process, the caterpillar seemingly kills itself and becomes an unrecognizable mush. But this death is the very thing that creates the protein-rich chowder that fuels the quick cell division forming all the parts of what makes an exquisite butterfly!

This is the way our healing comes as well. In an attempt to heal our woundedness, we become hungry and attempt to get our fill. Eventually, we become tired of our gluttonous ways, and in our self-reflection, we begin the slow, painful dying to self. It can be an agonizing demise of letting go of the things that have brought us comfort and peace but have blocked our ability to heal. This is the part of the healing process where we become scared of goodness and our own glory.

Here we must keep our eyes on the glorious resurrection after the required season of crucifixion. In this death we become pulp while creating the nourishing attributes that we need to become who God has always known we are. This is the aching beauty of healing change.

As we get used to our newfound beauty, we begin to exist differently in our world. Butterflies not only look more stunning than caterpillars but also behave differently. Likewise, we become new, not because pain is absent but because we have peace with its presence. We have more authenticity, more confidence, more sorrow, and more joy. We experience a rootedness that comes with knowing who we are. This is the beautiful mess of how we change. Because of God within us, transformative healing is not only possible but also attainable.

Wholeness is offered freely to us, but it is not guaranteed. There is, in fact, an evil one trying to steer us off course from being brought back to life out of the death we've wandered into, whether from chasing escape and easy relief or from letting bitterness and perfectionism take root. But if we persevere through the deaths we experience, we will find on the other side a father welcoming us back to life and setting a table for us, assuring us that everything he has is ours and helping us live into lives characterized no longer by death but by life to the full.

In conclusion, I offer you this blessing as you continue to grow in valor, stumbling toward wholeness:

> *May the peace of the Lord Christ go with you: wherever*
> *he may send you;*
> *may he guide you through the wilderness: protect you*
> *through the storm;*
> *may he bring you home rejoicing: at the wonders he*
> *has shown you;*
> *may he bring you home rejoicing: once again into*
> *our doors.*[6]

Let it be.

DISCUSSION QUESTIONS

Where in your life do you think you deny resurrection (an invitation to new life) because you deny suffering?

Where do you need to press more deeply into resurrection by living in truth? In what ways are you hiding?

What does personal resurrection look like for you at this stage of your journey? Where do you hope it will take you?

Pray and ask God to reveal what you need to "loosen your grip" on your life. What are you holding too tightly?

NOTES

INTRODUCTION: STUMBLING TOWARD WHOLENESS

1. Johannes Baptist Metz, *Poverty of Spirit* (Mahwah, NJ: Paulist Press, 1998), 4–5.
2. Henri Nouwen, *The Return of the Prodigal Son: A Story of Homecoming* (New York: Doubleday, 1994), 19–20.
3. Nouwen, 120–21.

CHAPTER ONE: BATTLING AFFECTIONS GONE MAD

1. See, for example, James W. Phillips, *The One Another Principles: a Biblical Blueprint for Small Group Fellowships* (Lima, OH: CSS Publishing, 2004), 184.
2. Kenneth E. Bailey, *Jacob and the Prodigal: How Jesus Retold Israel's Story* (Downers Grove, IL: IVP Academic, 2003), 95.
3. Henri Nouwen, *The Return of the Prodigal Son: A Story of Homecoming* (New York: Doubleday, 1994), 43.
4. Dan Allender, "Faith, Hope, Love" (lecture, Seattle School of Theology and Psychology, Seattle, WA, October 8, 2007).
5. Tom Stafford, "Drug Addiction: The Complex Truth," BBC, September 10, 2013, http://www.bbc.com/future/story/20130910-drug-addiction-the -complex-truth.
6. Lee N. Robins et al., "Vietnam Veterans Three Years after Vietnam: How Our Study Changed Our View of Heroin," *American Journal on Addictions* 19, no. 3 (May–June 2010): 203–11.

CHAPTER TWO: EXPOSING OUR SHAME

1. José Pinto-Gouveia and Marcela Matos, "Can Shame Memories Become a Key to Identity? The Centrality of Shame Memories Predicts

Psychopathology," *Applied Cognitive Psychology* 25, no. 2 (March–April 2011): 281–90; Diana Cândea and Aurora Szentagotai, "Shame and Psychopathology: From Research to Clinical Practice," *Journal of Cognitive and Behavioral Psychotherapies* 13, no. 1 (March 2013): 97–109.

2. Brené Brown, *Daring Greatly: How the Courage to Be Vulnerable Transforms the Way We Live, Love, Parent, and Lead* (New York: Avery, 2015), 68-69.

3. Brown, *Daring Greatly*, 73.

4. Brené Brown, "Listening to Shame," TED Talk, March 2012, 13:45/6:42, https://www.ted.com/talks/brene_brown_listening_to_shame.

5. See, for example, Brené Brown, "Shame Resilience Theory: A Grounded Theory Study on Women and Shame," *Families in Society: The Journal of Contemporary Social Services* 87, no. 1 (2006): 43–52.

6. K. Jessica Van Vliet, "Shame and Resilience in Adulthood: A Grounded Theory Study," *Journal of Counseling Psychology* 55, no. 2 (2008): 233–45.

7. Marianne Williamson, *A Return to Love: Reflections on the Principles of a Course in Miracles* (New York: HarperCollins, 1996), 191.

8. Frederick Buechner, *Telling Secrets: A Memoir* (repr., New York: HarperCollins, 2000), 35–36.

9. Emily Ochsenschlager, "Zora Neale Hurston Captured Essence of Blackness," NPR, February 23, 2011, https://www.npr.org/2011/02/23/133996265/Zora-Neale-Hurston-Captured-Essence-Of-Blackness.

10. Frederick Buechner, *Whistling in the Dark: A Doubter's Dictionary* (San Francisco: HarperCollins, 1993), 5.

11. Robert Augustus Masters, *To Be a Man: A Guide to True Masculine Power* (Boulder, CO: Sounds True, 2015), xvii.

12. Laurie Charles, "100 Creatives: Rune Lazuli Inspires Thousands with Her Words," *Miami New Times*, December 8, 2016, http://www.miaminewtimes.com/arts/100-creatives-rune-lazuli-inspires-thousands-with-her-words-8976638.

13. Bessel van der Kolk, *The Body Keeps the Score: Brain, Mind, and Body in the Healing of Trauma* (New York: Penguin Books, 2015), 98–99.

CHAPTER THREE: CONFRONTING OUR SELF-CONTEMPT

1. Andrew Ide, "The Devastation of Contempt," *The Allender Center* (blog), February 12, 2013, https://theallendercenter.org/2013/02/the-devastation-of-contempt/.

2. Chuck DeGroat, "On Self-Compassion, Inner Critics, and Becoming the Beloved—Part 1," *The New Exodus* (blog), August 19, 2011, https://chuckdegroat.net/2011/08/19/on-self-compassion-inner-critics-and-becoming-the-beloved-part-1/.

3. Robert Augustus Masters, *To Be a Man: A Guide to True Masculine Power* (Boulder, CO: Sounds True, 2015), xvii.

4. Andrew Ide, "New Series: Contempt & Blessing," *The Allender Center* (blog), October 5, 2012, https://theallendercenter.org/2012/10/new-series-blessing -contempt/.

CHAPTER FOUR: WRESTLING WITH GOODNESS

1. Richard Rohr, "Following the Mystics through the Narrow Gate" (lecture, Center for Action and Contemplation Conference, Albuquerque, NM, January 2010).

2. Timothy Keller, *The Prodigal God: Recovering the Heart of the Christian Faith* (New York: Riverhead Books, 2011), 21–22.

3. Encyclopedia.com, s.v. "kezazah," accessed March 27, 2018, https://www .encyclopedia.com/religion/encyclopedias-almanacs-transcripts-and-maps /kezazah.

4. Kenneth E. Bailey, *Jacob and the Prodigal: How Jesus Retold Israel's Story* (Downers Grove, IL: IVP, 2003), 102.

5. Bailey, *Jacob*, 103.

6. Dan Allender, *The Healing Path: How the Hurts in Your Past Can Lead You to a More Abundant Life* (Colorado Springs: WaterBrook, 2000), 21.

7. C. S. Lewis, *The Weight of Glory* (Grand Rapids, MI: Zondervan, 2001), 26.

8. Dan Allender, "Why We Sabotage Endings," *The Allender Center* (podcast), May 3, 2015, https://theallendercenter.org/2015/05/sabotage/.

9. Richard Rohr, *Things Hidden: Scripture as Spirituality* (Cincinnati, OH: Franciscan Media, 2008), 25.

CHAPTER FIVE: DEMANDING OUR DUE

1. "Devotionals: October 10–14, 2016" (Friday), Glenkirk Church, accessed March 27, 2018, http://www.glenkirkchurch.org/sermons-resources /devotions/devotionals-october-10-14-2016/.

2. Brad H. Young, *The Parables: Jewish Tradition and Christian Interpretation* (Grand Rapids, MI: Baker Academic, 2008), 138.

3. Paulo Coelho, *The Alchemist* (San Francisco: HarperOne, 2014), 18.

4. Dietrich Bonhoeffer, *The Cost of Discipleship* (New York: Touchstone, 1995), 185.

5. Alex Korb, *The Upward Spiral: Using Neuroscience to Reverse the Course of Depression, One Small Change at a Time* (Oakland, CA: New Harbinger, 2015), 158.

CHAPTER SIX: OWNING OUR CONTEMPT FOR OTHERS

1. Dan Allender, *The Wounded Heart: Hope for Adult Victims of Childhood Sexual Abuse* (Colorado Springs: NavPress, 2008), 83.
2. Paul Nuechterlein, "Fourth Sunday in Lent—Year C," *Girardian Lectionary*, March 9, 2016, http://girardianlectionary.net/reflections/year-c/lent4c/.
3. Brad H. Young, *Jesus: The Jewish Theologian* (Grand Rapids, MI: Baker Academic, 2011), 148.
4. Timothy Keller, *The Prodigal God: Recovering the Heart of the Christian Faith* (New York: Riverhead Books, 2011), 30.
5. Robert Augustus Masters, *To Be a Man: A Guide to True Masculine Power* (Boulder, CO: Sounds True, 2015), 80.
6. Masters, *To Be a Man*, 80.
7. Frederick Buechner, *Wishful Thinking: A Theological ABC* (New York: Harper & Row, 1973), 11.
8. Frederick Buechner, *Wishful Thinking: A Seeker's ABC* (San Francisco: HarperOne, 1993), 28.

CHAPTER SEVEN: ADDRESSING ABANDONMENT AND BETRAYAL

1. John and Stasi Eldredge, *Captivating: Unveiling the Mystery of a Woman's Soul* (revised and expanded ed.) (Nashville: Thomas Nelson, 2011), 71.
2. Dr. Brown made this comment in a theology class at Reformed Theological Seminary (Atlanta, GA, 2006).
3. Dorothy Day, "In Peace Is My Bitterness Most Bitter," *Catholic Worker* 33, no. 4 (January 1967): 2.

CHAPTER EIGHT: GRIEVING OUR WOUNDS

1. Paul Nuechterlein, "Fourth Sunday in Lent—Year C," *Girardian Lectionary*, March 9, 2016, http://girardianlectionary.net/reflections/year-c/lent4c/.
2. Barbara Brown Taylor, *Learning to Walk in the Dark* (San Francisco: HarperOne, 2014), 80.
3. C. S. Lewis, *The Four Loves* (New York: HarperCollins, 2017), 155–56.
4. Matt Williams, "The Prodigal Son's Father Shouldn't Have Run!: Putting Luke 15:11-32 in Context," *Biola*, summer 2010, accessed May 16, 2018, http://magazine.biola.edu/article/10-summer/the-prodigal-sons-father-shouldnt-have-run/.
5. James Coffield, "What Shame Does," *Tabletalk*, April 1, 2015, https://www.ligonier.org/learn/articles/what-shame-does/.
6. Friedrich Nietzsche, *Thus Spoke Zarathustra: A Book for Everyone and Nobody* (New York: Oxford University Press, 2009), 35.

7. "Rumi: Quotes: Quotable Quote," goodreads, accessed March 27, 2018, https://www.goodreads.com/quotes/983605-this-silence-this-moment-every-moment-if-it-s-genuinely-inside).

CHAPTER NINE: ENGAGING KINDNESS

1. Sam Jolman, "The Worst Motive for Change," *And Sons* magazine, no. 14, May 2015, http://andsonsmagazine.com/14/worst-motive-change#.Wlp RACOZOt8.
2. Henri Nouwen, *The Return of the Prodigal Son: A Story of Homecoming* (New York: Doubleday, 1994), 40.
3. Dan Allender, *Healing the Wounded Heart: The Heartache of Sexual Abuse and the Hope of Transformation* (Grand Rapids, MI: Baker, 2016), 143.

CHAPTER TEN: EMBRACING RESURRECTION

1. David Kinnaman, "The Porn Phenomenon," *Barna* (blog), February 5, 2016, http://www.barna.com/the-porn-phenomenon/#.VqZoN_krIdU.
2. Kinnaman, "Porn Phenomenon."
3. M. Scott Peck, *The Road Less Traveled: A New Psychology of Love, Traditional Values, and Spiritual Growth*, 25th anniversary ed. (New York: Touchstone, 2003), 50.
4. "Frontotemporal Dementia," Mayo Clinic, accessed April 30, 2018, https://www.mayoclinic.org/diseases-conditions/frontotemporal-dementia/symptoms-causes/syc-20354737.
5. Ted Loder, *Guerrillas of Grace: Prayers for the Battle* (Minneapolis: Augsburg Fortress, 2005), 55.
6. Shane Claiborne, Jonathan Wilson-Hartgrove, and Enuma Okoro, *Common Prayer: A Liturgy for Ordinary Radicals* (Grand Rapids, MI: Zondervan, 2010), 53.